Nothing Is Off the Table

Nothing Is Off the Table

A Radical Guide to Desire, Pleasure and Sexual Empowerment

Dr. Tiffany Stanley

Nothing Is Off the Table

Published by Tiffany Stanley Therapy
500 Grace Ln, Austin, TX 78746, United States

ISBN-979-8-234-02348-3

www.tiffanystanleytherapy.com

First Edition 2026

Printed in the United States of America

1 3 5 8 9 8 6 4 2

For the women who came before me, the women present with me today, and the women I have had the honor to support through therapy, whose lessons—spoken and unspoken—teach me to question, to grow, and to rise above societal limitations and the myths handed down through generations.

And especially for my sons, Cal and Camp, who have grown into beautiful, strong, and resilient men—men I am beyond proud of—and for my grandsons, Benjamin and James. They remind me daily that truth is a legacy worth protecting. This book is for all of you, and for all the generations yet to come, so that you may inherit truth instead of limits, possibility instead of fear, and stories illuminated—not shadowed—by the past.

About the Guided Meditations & Illustrations

The guided meditations in this book are offered for you to use in the way that feels most supportive. You may choose to record them in your own voice, or to be guided.

Audio versions, recorded by me, are available on my website.

The illustrations included in Chapter 5 were created by Emily Garrett of E. Garrett Designs.

You may access the recordings and learn more about the artist by scanning the QR codes below.

@EGARRETT_DESIGNS

Guided Meditations
& Resources

Contents

Introduction

Welcome to *Nothing Is Off the Table: A Radical Guide to Desire, Pleasure, and Sexual Empowerment*—a place where curiosity is welcome, messiness is expected, and pleasure has a seat saved just for you.

As a psychotherapist, sex therapist, and clinical sexologist, I have spent over twenty years sitting across from women, couples, and individuals in therapy rooms from Texas to the UK, listening to their stories. Genuine, sometimes confronting, often vulnerable stories. Stories that begin with exhaustion, confusion, or numbness and end with the reclaiming of something essential: *desire*.

This book emerged from these rich experiences, each an exploration into what it means to be a sexual being. From women who questioned if something was wrong with them because sex felt like a chore. From partners seeking connection but unsure where to begin—and from the countless brave souls who showed up, uncertain of what to say but deeply ready to feel something again.

Let's be clear from the start: This isn't a "how-to" guide for achieving perfect orgasms on command. It's not about fixing yourself—because you're not damaged. What it *is* about is exploring the beliefs, scripts, and habits that might be preventing you from accessing the pleasure, connection, and confidence you deserve.

In fact, many of us have been trying to cook from a sex recipe handed down by someone who didn't even like the dish. Generational scripts, cultural noise, and internalized shame can serve up a version of sexuality that leaves us cold. *Nothing Is Off the Table* invites you to clear the table and start again—with your own ingredients, your own appetite, and your own permission to savor.

We'll explore how desire manifests (and sometimes hides), how stress and life's chaos can lessen our sense of pleasure, and what it truly means to feel *safe* in our bodies and relationships. We'll take detours into visualization, breathwork, feminine energy, and a few playful metaphors about pantry cleanouts and tasty recipes for joy. And yes, sometimes sex will be the main course—and other times it will be a side dish to intimacy, connection, and self-awareness.

Throughout this journey, we will gently dismantle outdated myths. We'll shed light on debunked beliefs like your pleasure should align with someone else's schedule, you're too much—or not enough. We'll also challenge antiquated beliefs, such as the notion that your worth is tied to performance.

This book is for people who want more—not just more sex, but more *aliveness*. It's for couples who have drifted apart but still reach across the table. It's for anyone seeking to reconnect with their own body, to live with greater presence, permission, and joy.

You'll find stories, exercises, guided meditations, and questions that don't always have tidy answers. Because real change isn't linear. It's layered, slow-cooked, and often begins with asking the simplest question: *What do I really want?*

Nothing Is Off the Table isn't just a title—it's a philosophy. Here, there's space for your grief, hope, resistance, and curiosity. There's also room for laughter and awkwardness—and, ultimately, profound transformation. Within this book, my hope is that you discover ideas—and some effective tools—for the kind of intimacy that stirs your soul.

This is *your* invitation to take a seat at the table. Pull up a chair—what happens next might surprise you (and delight you!)

Chapter 1

Grandma's Outdated Cookbook

Somewhere along the way, amidst awkward health class discussions, whispered locker-room gossip, and romanticized Hollywood love scenes, we absorbed an unspoken message: *You're supposed to know everything about sex.*

Not just the mechanics of it, but the nuances—we enjoy, how to feel connected, how to ask, and how to feel good in our own skin. But most of us were handed cultural myths and outdated guidance in the form of Grandma's outdated cookbook, with torn pages and faded images. There was no proper index; "Pleasure" was listed somewhere between "Peril" and "Procreation," and the instructions were erroneous. The "recipe" most of us were given was missing half the steps and written in illegible handwriting. To make matters worse, the ingredients haven't changed since 1947.

Over the years, most of us were taught what *not* to do and what to *fear*. Little was spoken about curiosity, connection, or pleasure. School-based sex education focused less on learning and more on warnings, and archaic illustrations of the reproductive system paired with a healthy dose of shame. And movies? Hollywood portrays sex as effortless and perfect, never awkward, messy, or hesitant. We've also been taught that sex is natural, and because it's natural, it should be easy. But so is breathing, and even *that* can become complicated when anxiety arises.

The problem is that many of us are carrying around beliefs we never chose. Some were subtly handed to us ("nice girls don't . . ."), and others came wrapped in science-centric language we didn't understand. Still others are passed down through our genes, in a process called epigenetic transmission.* Think of it like this: If your grandmother endured war, scarcity, or constant criticism about her body, her nervous system learned to adapt just to survive. That adaptation—the vigilance, the scarcity mindset, the shame—can ripple through the family line even if no one ever says a word about it. It's like inheriting a family recipe card where the ingredients have been smudged and rewritten so many times you can't tell what the original dish was meant to be. You don't choose the smudges, but you still end up tasting them.

This doesn't mean we're doomed to carry the burdens of those who came before us. Epigenetics isn't a life sentence—it's a living script, and scripts can be rewritten. What was once written in stress and silence can be rewritten with safety, curiosity, and connection. When you notice yourself reacting with shame, fear, or disconnection, it might not be only *your* story. You could be feeling the reverberations of a story that started generations ago. The good news is that healing yourself can

---

* Epigenetic transmission can influence beliefs through the cross-generational inheritance of trauma-related stress responses, or the transmission of cultural continuity, which can be shaped by epigenetic mechanisms. Epigenetics, or the study of how behaviors and environment can change gene expression, means that experiences like stress or trauma can lead to changes that are passed down, potentially influencing a person's psychological responses and beliefs.

have ripple effects, too. When you pause, breathe, and choose a different response, you're not only creating freedom for yourself but also changing the script for those who come after you. Pleasure, safety, and openness become part of the inheritance. That's the power of awareness: We stop passing down the burnt casserole recipe and start offering something worth savoring instead.

These messages shaped our ideas of what is "normal" and what we expect from ourselves and our partners. They also made assumptions that we should already know everything there is to know about sex. But much of what we have been told—especially as women—is simply not accurate or helpful—and some is even harmful.

In this chapter, I'm going to call out some of those myths and offer alternatives to that timeworn, obsolete cookbook. Once you start seeing the myths for what they are, you can start replacing them with understanding, curiosity, and permission to rewrite the recipes on your own terms.

Myth #1—We Should *Just Know* How to Do This

In therapy, I often say, "We get the general gist" of what we are supposed to do when we have sex. We know what goes where (this body part goes into that body part), or at least we think we do—but that's about it. The rest? It's a wild mix of guessing and, unfortunately, in some cases, a "just get through it" mentality. And when it doesn't feel right or doesn't work, we assume something must be wrong.

Some of this stems from a lack of awareness of our bodies. It's not uncommon for clients in their thirties, forties, and beyond to tell me they've never looked at their own genitals— or that they still don't know how to describe what feels good, let alone how to ask for it. Many partners have no idea what triggers their loved one's body responses, and even less of an idea of how to begin that conversation. And why would they? The notion that sex is something we're just supposed to be good at, as if it were instinctual like blinking or sneezing, is one of the most harmful sexual myths we've inherited.

So, if you've ever thought you were the only one who didn't get it, or if you've wondered whether you somehow missed the secret lesson everyone else got, you aren't alone. Many of us walk around with gaps in our understanding because the myth was never questioned.

Sex is something we *learn*—and continue learning throughout life. Pleasure is something we *explore.* Understanding our bodies is a process, not a prerequisite. You aren't expected to know everything. But you *can* start learning everything that matters—regardless of where you are in life. And don't be ashamed of not knowing something. Just because you own a kitchen doesn't mean you know how to cook.

Myth #2—Sex Is Easy to Talk About— It's Natural, After All

Just because something is "natural" doesn't mean it's easy. Change is natural. So is aging. That doesn't mean we embrace them effortlessly.

Sex may be natural, but for most of us, talking about it is anything *but* comfortable. In fact, it can feel like one of the most vulnerable things we try to put into words. We're not just discussing physical acts—we're exploring desire, identity, pleasure, embarrassment, shame, insecurity, confusion, and maybe even grief. Not exactly light dinner conversation. We're addressing parts of ourselves we've often kept quiet or hidden—perhaps even from ourselves—and now we're expected to find words for all that and share it with someone else.

No wonder we freeze.

It's not uncommon for someone to tell me, "I don't even know what I like." Or: "I'm afraid to ask questions because I don't want to sound inexperienced." Beneath that, however, lies another unfounded, unspoken fear: *If I bring up sex, what will that say about me?*

We've inherited a tangle of messages about what it means to talk about sex: that if you're curious, it could be viewed as inappropriate; that if you ask, you must be unsatisfied—or if you don't already know, you must be behind. As a result, many people avoid the topic entirely—not because they aren't sexual, but because they're scared of what certain questions might reveal about them.

But here's the thing: Talking about sex doesn't mean you're doing it wrong. It means you care enough to want it to be better.

Think about this: *If you can't talk about it, you may not be ready to be doing it.* That's not a judgment—it's an invitation. If we're engaging in something as intimate and personal as sex, it makes sense to want some basic knowledge around it. The ability to be curious, and maybe wonder out loud, "What do *I* want?" is a great start.

Interestingly, being in a long-term relationship doesn't magically make these conversations easier. I've seen couples who've been together and having sex for twenty years, and they still haven't really *talked* about sex. They might be having it often—or rarely—but the topic itself? Still loaded, uncomfortable, and yes, mostly avoided.

Myth #3—Spontaneous Sex Is the Best Sex

Two people locked in eye contact pull each other into a kiss mid-sentence, stumble down a hallway, knocking over furniture along the way—to blissful, no-holds-barred sex. It's passionate, unplanned, and, according to the movies, it's the gold standard.

So when your real life resembles "Could we schedule sex for next Thursday?" it's natural to wonder if something's gone wrong.

The truth is that spontaneous sex is not the only kind of "good" sex. In fact, it's not even the most common type of good sex, and it's rarely as spontaneous as it appears. When we talk about planning sex, most people imagine it like planning a dentist appointment: stiff, clinical, and obligatory. But that's not what intentional intimacy has to be. I think of it as planning *an opportunity*—carving out time, space, and presence that makes intimacy more likely to happen. It's not about creating a step-by-step itinerary; it's about giving sex a place to land.

And what often shows up in that space is anticipation.

Think about the difference between throwing on clothes and rushing out for a last-minute dinner versus getting ready for a date. The time you take to prepare—to imagine how it might go, choose what to wear, think about where you'll meet, or what you might have to eat. That build-up? That's foreplay.

Intentionality isn't boring. It's brave. It says: *This matters enough to me that I want to create space for it.* Spontaneous sex sounds like it strikes out of nowhere—like a bolt of erotic lightning—but even the most "unplanned" sex usually starts with a cue. A glance. A memory. A moment of flirtation or a subtle body signal. Your brain picks up on something that turns it toward pleasure. That spark isn't magic—it's momentum. Which means you can create it, too.

When people say that spontaneous sex is the best sex, what they often remember is the feeling of surprise, of desire surfacing unannounced. But that doesn't mean planned sex is somehow "lesser than"—it just means you're setting the stage instead of hoping lightning strikes. Being intentional about sex isn't a symptom of a broken relationship; it's a sign of a thoughtful one.

Myth #4—Sex Is Only Sex When a Penis Enters a Vagina

We've been taught a narrow definition of what "counts" as sex. For many of us, it's been reduced to one course—penis-in-vagina intercourse—as if everything else is merely foreplay or somehow doesn't "qualify." However, sex is much more expansive than that. Oral sex, hand stimulation, touch, and closeness are all forms of sex. They are real, valid, and worthy in their own right.

Here is why that matters: Experiencing pain during intercourse or facing issues like erectile dysfunction or other physical limitations doesn't mean sex is off the table. Far from it. We can still have deeply satisfying sexual experiences—whether with a partner or by ourselves—by expanding our understanding of what intimacy can look like. Sometimes, when we stop pursuing a narrow definition of sex, we uncover possibilities that are not only accessible but may even be more pleasurable than what we once thought we were missing.

Myth #5—Men Are Always Ready for Sex, and Women Only Want Romance

We've all heard this myth: Men are purportedly thinking about sex 24/7—and always up for it. Meanwhile, women are often portrayed as the romantics, yearning for cuddles and a slow, sensual build-up. However, like most overly simplified stereotypes, this one doesn't hold up—and it does everyone a disservice. This notion is akin to saying men only crave fast food and women only desire candlelit dinners. In reality, most people enjoy both—depending on their mood.

Despite what we've been led to believe, men are not sex machines. They aren't always in the mood or automatically excited just because an opportunity arises. Like all of us, they're affected by mood, stress, fatigue, body image, and emotional connection—everything that comes with being human. When we assume they're always ready, it puts tremendous pressure on them to perform. If they're not immediately responsive, it can spark confusion for a partner: "*Am I not attractive enough? Are you not into me?*" But arousal doesn't operate on a switch—and for many men, the expectation to flip that switch may actually shut it down.

For women, the narrative suggests that we're only interested in emotional closeness or "romantic" sex. While emotional intimacy is important for many of us, it doesn't mean we don't crave a little excitement as well. Many of us appreciate spontaneity and seek something wild or unplanned.

The truth is that desire is diverse. There's no universal recipe for what turns someone on—not for men or women.

Assuming otherwise doesn't bring us closer to our partners or to ourselves; it merely reinforces outdated narratives that make everyone feel a little more alienated.

15

Myth #6—If You Don't Always Feel Love, Desire, or Attraction Toward Your Partner, Something Must Be Wrong with Your Relationship

Here's a little secret: Even in the healthiest, happiest relationships, love and desire aren't always on full blast. That feeling of "I can't get enough of you" waxes and wanes—for everyone. And despite what we've been taught, that doesn't mean there's anything wrong with us or our relationship.

Attraction and sexual interest are fluid. They are influenced by stress, hormones, body image, sleep, resentment, routine, and, yes, whether your partner has been especially irritating this week. Sometimes we don't feel close because we're burned out, or we've been marinating in the same stale routines for months. Other times, it's because we haven't seen each other outside of sweatpants in what feels like forever, causing the spark to get buried under logistics and laundry.

This doesn't mean we've fallen out of love. It doesn't mean we're broken, or that we need to chase a new partner just to feel alive again. It means we're living in the real world, where desire is responsive—it shifts based on what's happening around us and inside us. Feeling a dip in attraction is not a red flag— it's an invitation to be curious, not critical. It's also completely normal to miss that "new relationship energy" sometimes while still being deeply committed to your partner. Both can be true.

So let's stop pretending that real love means constant fireworks. Sometimes, it looks like a quiet Tuesday, making a new recipe together and choosing to stay connected even when desire is snoozing. Just know that it *can* return, especially when we give ourselves the space to understand it rather than judge it.

Myth #7—Everyone Is Having More (and Better) Sex Than You

I'd genuinely like to know: *Who are these people?*

You know the ones—the mysterious masses we imagine engaging in wild, frequent, emotionally satisfying, technically flawless sex in well-lit rooms, with perfect bodies—where there's never anything awkward about it.

We compare ourselves to those elusive "others," even though we don't know who *they* are and have never seen them. Yet, when we really think about it, *we have no idea what anyone else's sex life actually looks like.*

But that doesn't stop the myth. We still look at our own experiences—whatever those may be—and ask, "Why don't I have what everyone else has?" Or worse, "What's wrong with me that I don't want sex as often as they seem to? Or that mine feels messier, or more complicated?"

Here's the uncomfortable truth: Most of us are only hearing the highlight reel. People tend to share the fun stuff, the wins, and the one-night stand described like a movie scene. Or they don't say much at all—except maybe when something goes wrong, and even then, it's shared like a confession, not a conversation.

That doesn't mean anyone is lying; it simply means people are curating. They present the aspects they believe will be interesting, funny, impressive, or relatable at that moment. You are hearing one carefully chosen slice of someone's reality —not the full meal.

Sometimes, we all need to feel a little better about ourselves, and sex stories—true or not—can serve as a form of ego-boosting PR. However, the problem isn't other people's stories. The issue arises when we use them as a measure of our own worth.

This is the real heart of the myth: The belief that ease, frequency, and performance are the metrics that define sexual success. That if you're not having sex often—or loving it every time—something must be broken. That "everyone else" is doing it better, more, happier, and without any obstacles.

That's not only false; it's cruel. It reduces sex to a competition rather than a connection. So the next time your brain presents that unhelpful story—"Everyone else is having great sex but me"—try asking: *What am I assuming? What don't I know?* Then remind yourself that no one gets a gold star for frequency. There is no secret society of sexually superior humans. There are just people figuring it out, one imperfect moment at a time.

Myth #8—Sex Is Only for the Young, Beautiful, and Thin

There's a quiet yet persistent cultural narrative that tells us sex has an expiration date. Upon reaching a certain age—or a specific dress size—you're expected to silently retire your libido, fold away your desire, and retreat into invisibility. As if sex belongs solely to the young, smooth-skinned, flexible, and flawless. And as if pleasure ceases at some arbitrary age, or once gravity begins to take effect.

Let's break that myth wide open. People of all ages, shapes, sizes, and mobility levels are having sex. Great sex. Loving sex. And sometimes awkward sex. And they're definitely not all doing it by candlelight, wearing luxurious, wildly expensive lingerie. They're doing it in their real bodies—the ones with scars, softness, and stories—and they're also enjoying it.

Here's a fact that might surprise you: Some of the highest rates of sexually transmitted infections are found in nursing homes. Not because older people are reckless—but because they're having sex. Often, they hold the mistaken belief that STIs only pose a risk to the young, or that post-menopausal bodies are somehow immune. (Spoiler alert: They're not.)

But the larger point here is that sex doesn't belong to a specific body type or age group. It belongs to *you*. It reflects how you feel in your own skin and what you wish to experience—whether you're twenty-eight or seventy-eight, whether you wear a size 2 or a size 22.

Many people say things like, "I'll feel sexy when I lose weight," or "I can't imagine being naked in front of someone right now." I understand that. But that's like saying, "I can't go to the gym because I'm not already fit." You don't need to earn access to sex by meeting a beauty standard. Sex isn't reserved for those who already feel perfect—it's one of the ways we can *reconnect* with our bodies and find pleasure in them, just as they are.

Something else happens when you give yourself permission to be fully in your body during sex—especially as you age or grow into a new version of yourself. You begin to realize that feeling sexy isn't about looking a certain way; it's about being present, feeling good, and reclaiming joy.

You don't have to wait for someone else to declare your body worthy of pleasure. You can affirm it now and then demonstrate it to yourself.

Myth #9—If a Man Loses His Erection, He's Not into You Anymore

Let's clear this up: Erections are not on/off switches. They're not light bulbs. They're not "yes" or "no." They resemble waves—fluid, responsive, sometimes strong, sometimes subtle, and sometimes . . . taking a break.

Yet many people believe that if a penis isn't constantly erect during a sexual encounter, something must be wrong. They think the man isn't interested anymore, that the sex is over, or worse—that it's a failure.

Here's the reality: Erections naturally ebb and flow. That's not dysfunction—it's blood flow. It's biology. Erections don't happen in a straight line; they are a dynamic experience influenced by many factors—physical, mental, emotional, and relational.

So what happens when that natural ebb shows up? Often, panic sets in. The internal narrative is: *It's over. I've failed.* And panic is the fastest way to shut down arousal altogether. This is the cycle of performance anxiety—when the fear of not having an erection becomes the very thing that prevents it.

But if we could reframe it—if we saw it not as the end, but as a pause, or a shift, or a moment to reattune—then we'd start treating sex like the fluid, responsive thing it truly is. Arousal—and eventually orgasm—is more like slow roasting than a microwave. It builds with warmth and time, not just a push of a button.

And here's another myth tangled in this one: The sign of "great sex" is a constant erection, constant lubrication, and simultaneous orgasms. But that's a cinematic fantasy—not a human standard. In real life, arousal fluctuates. Bodies shift and sensations change. Lubrication is not always a dependable sign of arousal, and orgasms are not the only—or even best—measure of pleasure.

You know what a good indicator is? Presence. The connection we feel with our partner, the curiosity about what we could do differently, and the pleasure from the sensations we experience. Sometimes there's an erection the whole time, and other times there isn't. None of that means something's wrong.

Men can orgasm without an erection. Women can enjoy sex without copious lubrication. And partners of any gender can experience real connection even when their bodies do not adhere to the so-called script.

Of course, when there are ongoing challenges with arousal or function, it's important to consult with a healthcare provider. However, remember that these aren't moral failings—they're issues that can be addressed and supported.

Instead of measuring sex by how hard, wet, or orgasmic it is, perhaps it's time to gauge it by how *true* it feels—how attuned you are to your own experience and your partner's. Because sex doesn't need to be perfect to be worth having; it just needs to be real.

Myth #10—If a Man Loses His Erection, It Means He Has Erectile Dysfunction

As another aspect of Myth #9, let's begin with the obvious: Losing an erection *once in a while* is not the same as having erectile dysfunction.

But many men experience a single moment of softness and immediately panic—*What's wrong with me? Will this keep happening?* That anxiety can trigger a cycle of worry, pressure, and overanalysis that exacerbates the problem.

Here's the truth: At some point in life, every man will face some difficulty getting or maintaining an erection. This is part of being human, not a sign of permanent dysfunction.

Sometimes it's stress. Sometimes it's fatigue. Sometimes it's timing. Sometimes it's simply that the brain and body aren't on the same page that day. However, what often turns a minor moment into a recurring struggle is the meaning attached to it.

Instead of thinking, *Okay, this happens sometimes,* many men jump straight to, *This means something is wrong with me* . . . which then leads to performance anxiety. The fear of it happening again becomes so strong that it *does* happen again. Not because of a medical issue, but because the body doesn't respond well to pressure and fear.

From there, things can spiral. Will my partner be disappointed, rejected, or, worse, angry? Will they think I'm not attracted to them? Then all that fear and shame tighten the grip of angst, and anxiety and arousal don't exactly make great bedfellows.

That said, if erection challenges persist, it's important to approach the situation with curiosity rather than fear. Factors such as testosterone levels, blood circulation, medications, chronic illnesses, thyroid function, or even alcohol consumption can contribute to the problem. Your doctor can help identify these factors. However, it's also possible that the issue is rooted in mental or emotional aspects—stress, relationship dynamics, performance pressure, or fear of failure may also be the cause.

So no—losing an erection isn't automatically a sign of dysfunction. It's a moment—maybe a message. Sometimes it's asking you to slow down or inviting a conversation. Other times, it's just a brief occurrence, with no significant meaning whatsoever.

What matters is how we respond: with fear and self-blame, or with compassion and curiosity?

Myth #11—Sex Dies in Long-Term Relationships

It's present in sitcoms, stand-up routines, and sighs at dinner tables everywhere: Once you move in together, get married, or have kids, your sex life is officially over—as if commitment is the ultimate libido killer and domesticity the foe of desire.

And absolutely, there are seasons in life when sex becomes quiet. When sleep feels more urgent than seduction, especially when parenting stretches you thin. Sometimes work demands your attention, your body is exhausted, and the laundry has piled up again. None of that means desire disappears, and it certainly doesn't mean that a committed relationship is a death sentence for your sex life.

What usually happens is this: Intentionality fades. People stop creating space for intimacy, not because they don't care, but because they assume *this is just how it is now.* The myth gets internalized. Instead of noticing the shift and talking about it, they settle into quiet acceptance. The silence and disconnection grow, and the myth starts to look true—not because it was inevitable, but because no one questioned it.

Here's what is *actually* true: Desire in long-term relationships requires nurturing, not performance or perfection. Just care and intention. Just like we schedule time to cook a meal, go to the gym, or walk the dog, there are times when we need to be intentional about connection. (See Myth #3.) And when we do, we're not "forcing" anything. We're creating space for it to happen.

Sex doesn't vanish just because two people fall in love or sign a lease. It fades away when it's no longer nurtured—when discussions about it become too awkward to have, or when stress and routine push it to the bottom of the priority list.

But the capacity for connection, pleasure, and intimacy doesn't disappear. It may simply be waiting to be invited back in.

Myth #12—Women Take Too Long to Orgasm

Too long according to . . . what?

This myth is based on a timeline that was never designed for women in the first place. It relies on how quickly *men* tend to orgasm during sex and assumes that anything longer, slower, or more layered is somehow an inconvenience—as if pleasure should adhere to a stopwatch.

In reality, there's no such thing as "too long" when it comes to orgasm. There's just your body doing what it does, in its own time and under its own unique set of conditions. Comparing that to someone else's pace is like judging a sunrise against a sparkler. They're both beautiful, but they evolve at a different pace.

The problem is that most statistics we hear about female orgasm—like "only X percent of women orgasm from intercourse"—lack context. *What kind* of intercourse? What position? What type of stimulation (if any) is occurring simultaneously? Was there touch . . . foreplay? Was there clitoral contact? Was she mentally present? Did she feel safe? Desired? Most of these studies also define "intercourse" narrowly—as vaginal penetration with no additional stimulation. This definition doesn't accurately represent how most people actually experience sex—or pleasure.

When women hear stats like "most women can't orgasm during intercourse," they internalize the wrong message. It's not that the definition of sex is too limited or that pleasure looks different for every body; rather, they believe *they* are taking too long and therefore that something is wrong with them. This may lead to the assumption that they're difficult, demanding, or disappointing.

This leads to another cycle: the pressure to "hurry up." There is a fear of being "too much." There is a worry that your partner will lose interest or get bored. So, instead of tuning in, women often tune out—trying to make it quick and *perform* pleasure rather than feel it.

But here's the thing: Orgasm is not a deadline. It isn't a test. The notion that it must occur within a specific time frame to be valid is entirely false.

The truth is that orgasm takes as long as it takes. Sometimes it's minutes, and sometimes it doesn't happen at all. And that's okay. When the pressure is released, the possibility usually increases. What leads to orgasm varies from person to person. Even for the same person, it can shift from day to day depending on stress, mood, physical comfort, emotional connection, hormone levels, and myriad other invisible factors. That's not dysfunction; that's being human.

The question isn't, "*Why does it take so long?*" The question is, "*What helps me feel good?*"

It's not that women take too long; it could simply be because the "oven" was never preheated.

Myth #13—It's Your Partner's Job to Turn You On

We all want our partners to know exactly what to say, how to touch us, and how to set the mood—maybe with the perfect playlist, a sly look, or a well-timed shoulder squeeze. We long to feel desired. And sometimes, they do just that. However, expecting your partner to be solely responsible for your arousal or pleasure is a bit like expecting someone else to do your stretching before a workout.

This myth—that your partner should "make" you want sex, "give" you an orgasm, or "figure out" what gets you going—is one of the most persistent detours away from achieving true sexual fulfillment.

Because the reality is that arousal *begins within you*. It's influenced by your mindset, your relationship with your body, your ability to stay present, and your willingness to explore. While a partner can certainly enhance, amplify, respond to, and co-create pleasure, they cannot be in charge of it.

You'd be surprised by how many people believe that "if my partner loved me enough," or "if they were more fun/attentive," they'd automatically know how to get everything going. But partners aren't mind readers. They can't guess what feels good if *we* don't know—or don't say. That's not selfishness; it's communication. It's also a collaboration. Doesn't that sound more empowering?

The same goes for orgasm. It's easy to fall into the belief that if your partner just does enough touching or trying, then an orgasm will happen. But orgasm isn't a prize someone else hands you. It's something that unfolds when the body and mind are on the same team. If your internal script says, "This never works for me," or "I can't," or "I shouldn't need this," it's going to be hard for any amount of external stimulation to override that.

But when you shift your attention inward—toward sensation and curiosity, toward noticing what *feels* good rather than what *should* be happening—everything changes. Suddenly, the experience itself becomes worthwhile, whether or not it concludes with fireworks.

Pleasure doesn't have to be a solo mission. However, it starts with you, and keep in mind that your partner can't guess; so make sure to communicate what's working.

Myth #14—Your Partner *Gave* You That Orgasm

This one closely follows the last myth, and for good reason. We've all heard it—or maybe said it ourselves: "*I gave her a great orgasm.*" It's often expressed with pride, sometimes with a wink, and occasionally with a full-on victory lap.

But here's the truth: No one "gives" you an orgasm like a beautifully wrapped present. That's not how pleasure works.

Orgasm is a function your body *performs*. It's a physiological, psychological, and deeply personal experience that can be supported, co-created, and invited—but cannot be handed over. And certainly not controlled by someone else.

Now, that doesn't mean your partner plays no role—of course they do. A good lover is responsive, attentive, and tuned in. But your orgasm doesn't belong to them. It belongs to *you*—your ability to feel and stay present, to be turned on, and to let go. Trust what's happening. Your partner can help facilitate the experience, but they are not the sole architect of it.

It's somewhat like saying that someone made you laugh. Certainly, their joke was the catalyst—but your laughter originated from *you*. It surged through your body. Your mind registered it. Your body reacted. The same applies to orgasm.

The issue with saying "he gave me an orgasm" or "I gave her one" is that it places all the power—and often all the pressure—in the hands of someone else. It implies a level of control that doesn't truly exist. Worse, it reinforces the notion that good sex is something that's *done to you*, instead of something you actively participate in. It also leads to some pretty shaky self-esteem. If you're the one who's "giving" orgasms, you might start tying your worth as a lover to someone else's response—something you can't actually control. And if you're not having orgasms, it's easy to feel like your partner is failing you—or that you're failing.

Pleasure is a partnership. Yes, your partner's presence matters, as does yours. You can have an orgasm while your partner is doing all the right things—or none of them. You might be touched in exactly the same way on two different days, yielding two totally different outcomes. It's not just about technique; it's about context. It's about *you*.

Myth #15—A Healthy Sexual Relationship Means We're Always on the Same Page

There's a persistent idea that in a healthy sexual relationship, both partners should have the *same level* of desire, the *same frequency* of interest, and the *same readiness* at the *same time.* Sounds tidy. However, this is not how real people operate.

In nearly every relationship, one partner tends to have a higher level of desire than the other. Sometimes this remains consistent. Other times, it shifts over time. It can also be contextual—linked to stress, hormones, health, and life stages. This doesn't mean your relationship is damaged; it means you're human. It's not about being perfectly matched; it's about being willing to meet each other where you are.

Desire is not a personality trait; it's not something you're either "good" or "bad" at. It's responsive and relational, often changing not only between people but also within a single person from day to day.

We get into trouble when we start believing that matched desire equals emotional compatibility—or that mismatched desire means someone isn't attracted anymore or that something has gone wrong. Those assumptions create distance, resentment, and shame.

What if we approached the difference with curiosity instead? Rather than saying, "We're out of sync, so something must be wrong," try asking:

> What does desire look like for me?
> What builds it? And what blocks it?
> Are we both feeling seen, heard, and valued—
> even if our interest levels are different right now?

Here's another important truth: Sometimes you're not interested from the start. That doesn't mean you won't become interested. Responsive desire—the kind that shows up after connection begins—is just as valid as spontaneous desire. You don't need to be immediately turned on to be open to intimacy.

The healthiest sexual partnerships aren't the ones where both people always want the same thing simultaneously. They're the ones where differences aren't feared or resented; instead, they're respected, understood, and navigated. Real connection isn't about matching every craving—it's about making space for each other's rhythms and finding pleasure in the mix.

Myth #16—It's the Man's Job to Initiate Sex

He's the pursuer, the one with the ever-present desire, the one who knocks on the bedroom door with a raised eyebrow and perhaps a caress or a passionate kiss. Meanwhile, the woman is meant to be responsive, mysterious, and maybe even reluctant—until she's "won over."

For generations, we've been fed the idea that it's the man's role to initiate sex. This script is outdated and not working for a lot of people.

The truth is that anyone can initiate sex. In healthy relationships, both partners *should* feel empowered to initiate—not just because it's more equitable, but because it communicates something deeper: *I see you. I desire you.*

When women don't initiate—not because they don't want to, but because they feel it's not their role—it creates an imbalance. One partner ends up carrying all the pressure of pursuit, while the other may wait, hoping their partner somehow *knows* when the moment feels right.

But desire doesn't work well with assumption; it works best with clarity. And that's where communication comes in—not just about who initiates, but how.

Initiation doesn't always look the same for everyone. For some, being pursued is part of their arousal. The feeling of being wanted, sought after, and invited into intimacy—that's a turn-on. For others, taking the initiative feels exciting and powerful. There's no right or wrong way to feel about it. However, it *does* help to talk about it.

What excites you more—taking the initiative or being approached? How do you prefer to be invited into intimacy?

What signals resonate with you, and which ones miss the mark?

Let's be honest—some forms of initiation are more successful than others. I often hear: "My husband walked in and squeezed my butt, and that was supposed to be my signal." It might be playful or familiar, but if it's not *received* as an invitation to intimacy, then it's not achieving its intended purpose. And if it feels juvenile or out of sync with your mood, it may have the opposite effect entirely.

None of this means anyone is doing it "wrong." It just indicates that what feels like initiation to one person may not register the same way with another. So, if we're not communicating, we're just guessing—and often getting it wrong.

Myth #17—The Best Lovers Only Focus on Their Partner's Pleasure

We often romanticize the selfless lover—the one who gives unconditionally and knows exactly what you like. They prioritize their partner's pleasure, leaving their own at the door. This kind of generosity can seem both noble and very sexy.

Sex, like a perfect meal, isn't just about serving someone else—it's about savoring it together. Likewise, the most connected and satisfying sexual experiences occur when both partners are attuned to each other and themselves.

When your attention is solely on your partner's feelings, desires, and how they're responding, you may become disconnected from your own sensations. Your partner might enjoy themselves thoroughly—and you might even climax. However, the experience can begin to feel more like performance than genuine presence.

Pleasure isn't a one-way street. It's a shared space—one that becomes richer and more textured when both people contribute. It's not just about technique; it's also about awareness.

When you are in tune with your body—what excites you, what feels pleasurable, what you're longing for—you contribute more to the experience. You're not merely going through the motions of what typically works or what your partner enjoys; you're incorporating the full spectrum of your own desires. That's not selfish—it's intimate and responsive. It's also authentic.

Of course, it's lovely to know your partner's favorite position or how to touch them in a way that excites them. However, if you concentrate only on that, you might find yourself on autopilot—going through a familiar script instead of showing up for the moment.

When sex becomes too one-sided, even if it appears successful from the outside, it can start to feel unbalanced. You might feel appreciated—but not fully *seen*. Or generous—but not fully satisfied.

Great lovers don't just aim to please; they show up. They notice how you're feeling and how they are responding. They allow their own pleasure to be part of the experience, rather than something they're supposed to set aside for someone else's benefit.

Pleasure is more powerful when it's mutual.

Myth # 18—If a Woman Uses a Sex Toy, It Means Her Partner Isn't Enough

A sex toy is not a judgment or rejection of anyone—it's a tool. A vibrator is not a competitor; it's more like a supplement and, sometimes, just really good company. But somewhere along the line, sex toys—especially vibrators—became framed as substitutes rather than *enhancements*, as if the moment a woman reaches for one, she's making a statement: *You're not enough.*

But the truth is, using a sex toy doesn't mean your partner is lacking. It simply means you're exploring pleasure.

Even if the toy resembles a penis or mimics some function of partnered sex, it still isn't *replacing* a person, no matter how high-tech or anatomically correct it is. A toy can't kiss you (well, at least not one I know of . . .). It can't laugh with you, connect with you emotionally, respond to your breathing, or adapt to your shifting energy. A toy can't make love to you—it can stimulate you. Those are two very different things.

Human bodies and toys serve different purposes. A vibrator, for instance, can provide stimulation that is more consistent, intense, and quicker than a human partner ever could. And that's the point. It's not about replacing what someone can do—it's about *enhancing* your pleasure and sexual satisfaction.

People mistakenly believe that using a vibrator or sexual toy may desensitize you to stimulation and pleasure. That's completely false—unless you have used it excessively to the point of injuring nerve endings (ouch!). Most people can climax faster with a toy because it does things that a human can't. But that doesn't mean it is better than partner sex, or that there can't be a translation from one sexual mode to another, or that it can't be enjoyed *during* partner sex.

Toys can contribute to solo pleasure, partnered pleasure, exploration, or healing. They can help someone discover their preferences, achieve orgasm more easily, or simply feel more in control of their experience. In many cases, they can *enhance* intimacy with a partner—when used with trust, curiosity, and openness.

The only time toys become a threat is when they're misunderstood, such as when a partner feels left out or insecure. It's not because of what the toy is, but because of what they fear it signifies.

Questions to consider: *What role does this play for you? How can we make this part of our shared experience?* Or, *How do you feel about me exploring pleasure on my own?*

That's the difference between feeling replaced and feeling included. The bottom line is that a sex toy doesn't mean someone's not "good enough." It signifies that pleasure is being taken seriously. And that's something everyone deserves.

Myth #19—You Can Become Addicted to a Toy and Ultimately Be Unable to Have an Orgasm Without It

Similar to Myth #18, this myth has been unnecessarily perpetuated over the years. Many people genuinely believe they could become addicted to a toy and be unable to orgasm without a vibrator.

It's rare for someone to become "addicted" to a toy, but instead, what can happen is that a person can become reliant on using a toy to achieve an orgasm because they do not allow for exploration and variation, which helps us to learn different ways to reach an orgasm, including orgasms without the use of a toy.

So, if you use a toy, and that's typically how you're able to have an orgasm, try the vibrator in different places at different intensities. Try using your hands and allow for variety so you don't get attached to one thing and miss out on the opportunity to explore. There are numerous variations that feel enjoyable. All involve curious exploration, which is a very good thing.

Myth #20—You Should Know What Your Partner Wants and Needs Sexually, Because You Are Partners

If you're already having sex with someone, shouldn't you just *know* what they like? The idea that being in a relationship somehow grants you intuitive access to your partner's pleasure map is false. It's not true that if you're close, or if you love each other enough, the signals will be obvious. There's no need for awkward conversations, right? You'll just figure it out.

But here's the problem: Reading someone's body is not the same as knowing their mind. And assuming you "just know" what they want can lead you far away from what they actually enjoy.

Moans and movements can certainly offer clues, but they aren't always reliable. Sometimes people "fake it," presenting a performance of how they think they should respond, what they believe will seem sexy or enjoyable. This obviously gives inaccurate information to their partner, but the pressure to behave a certain way to appear sexy, sexually knowledgeable, or responsive (often based on messages and myths they've absorbed) can lead people to "play a part" instead of authentically being present. So, simply put, *be real*—even if it means not moaning, heavy breathing, or moving all over the place.

And if you think this is a "women-only" issue, think again. Men fake it, too, often for the same reasons: to avoid disappointing their partner, to speed things up, to mask discomfort or disconnection, or to escape the pressure of performance. The problem with faking isn't just that it creates a false moment; it creates a false road map. When someone pretends to enjoy something they're not really into, it teaches their partner to keep doing it. It reinforces an inaccurate idea of what pleasure means for them in that relationship.

Over time, this creates a cycle: the same motions, misunderstandings, and, ultimately, the same silence. Then, people wonder why their sex life feels disconnected or lackluster.

That's why communication matters. Not just before or after sex, but during it. Not just about what feels good, but also about what *doesn't*. Sometimes, the most respectful and intimate thing you can say is: "*This isn't really working for me—can we pause?*" Or, "*I'm not in the zone right now, but I'd love to try something different.*"

Being sexual with someone doesn't mean you know everything about them, nor does it mean they know everything about you. Desire isn't a guessing game—it's a conversation that continues to unfold over time. Even the best chefs don't guess what their guests want. Being in a relationship doesn't make you a mind reader; it simply means you're in the same kitchen. You still need to work through the recipe together.

Myth #21—If You Say No to Sex, You're Rejecting Your Partner

Saying no to sex can feel loaded, especially in a long-term relationship where we expect desire to be mutual and perfectly timed.

When one partner initiates and the other responds, "*I'm not really in the mood,*" it's easy for that moment to feel like a rejection—or evidence that something is amiss. One partner may even jump to the incorrect conclusion that they are undesirable.

Saying no to sex is not the same as saying no to your partner. It means saying no *to sex*—in that moment, in that mood, in that body. And it's important to be able to say no just as freely as we say yes, free of guilt and without resentment or obligation.

Sometimes a no is a "*not right now.*" Maybe because you're stressed, tired, or emotionally off. Perhaps your body isn't responding the way you want it to, or your head is miles away. These are all human experiences—not personal rejections.

If the answer is *always* no, then yes—that may indicate a need for deeper examination. However, that's a conversation about the relationship, not about the pressure to have sex.

Also, can we please completely retire the idea of sex as a "duty"? I've heard the phrases "wifely duty" or "it feels like a chore or a duty" far too often, and each time it reinforces the myth that one partner owes the other sex because of their role. That's not intimacy; that's obligation. And obligation is not a foundation for mutual pleasure.

The other thing to keep in mind is that sometimes arousal comes *after* initiation. You might start out as a *maybe*—not really in the mood, but open to seeing where things go. If things stay the same and you're not feeling it?

You can express that. It's not failure; it's genuine honesty.

Saying no is essential for a healthy sexual relationship. It indicates that you're listening to your body and trusting your partner enough to be genuine. Additionally, it fosters an environment where yes truly means *yes*—not "*I guess I should.*"

Myth #22—The Best Sex Happens in Your Twenties

It's a common belief—reinforced by movies, pop culture, and nostalgia—that the peak of your sex life occurs when you're young. Your twenties are when sex is at its most exciting, frequent, and passionate.

Here's a secret that anyone over thirty—and far beyond—usually already knows: **Most twenty-somethings don't really know what they're doing.** They're learning . . . figuring it out. They're driven by hormones, not always by clarity. They're often more focused on having the opportunity for sex rather than on *how they're feeling.* They may also be trying to unlearn shame, find their voice, and feel comfortable in their bodies.

That's not to say people in their twenties don't have good sex—they do. But good sex improves with age. Why? Because we start to understand ourselves. We know what feels good—and what doesn't. We've had more experiences, better communication, and a broader, more attuned perspective. And hopefully, we gain more confidence to express what we want and need.

As we age, sex often becomes less about performance and more about connection. It becomes less about following a pattern and more about exploring what's real. There's a shift away from proving something and toward actually *feeling* something. That kind of intimacy doesn't always reveal itself in our youth because it comes from growth.

Hormones change—but so does the quality of our attention. We may take things more seriously or more lightly, depending on the moment. We understand what matters and what doesn't, what holds meaning, and what excites us in ways that aren't always physical.

So no, your twenties are not the gold standard for your sexual peak. Not even close. The best sex isn't tied to age; it is linked to factors such as communication, safety, self-trust, emotional presence, and experiences. These aspects often strengthen over time.

Myth #23—If a Man Enjoys Anal Play, He Must Be Gay

This is one of those myths that's less about anatomy and more about assumptions. And like most assumptions about sex, it's wildly inaccurate and could even be construed as damaging. To start with anatomy: The prostate is one of the most erotically sensitive areas of the male body. Sometimes called the "male G-spot," it can produce intense pleasure when stimulated. This can be done externally, but direct internal stimulation—through anal play or penetration—is often the most effective way to access it. It has nothing to do with sexual orientation.

Enjoying prostate stimulation doesn't mean a man wants to have sex with another man. It means he has a body with nerve endings that respond to pressure and touch. That isn't a preference for a gender—it's a physiological reality. However, due to persistent cultural beliefs linking anal play with homosexuality, many men avoid exploring that aspect of their pleasure potential. They worry: *What does it mean if I like this? Will my partner think I'm gay?* This anxiety can shut down curiosity before it even begins. This is unfortunate because when men are shamed out of exploring what feels good in their own bodies, they miss out on a fuller, richer, and more embodied experience of sex. Pleasure becomes something they're allowed to have—just not *too much* of it. And definitely not in "certain" places.

Orientation refers to who you are attracted to, while pleasure pertains to what feels good in your body. The two concepts are not interchangeable. A man's desire to explore anal stimulation does not mean he is gay; rather, it indicates he is open to discovering more about what brings him pleasure. It's similar to cooking without a recipe—you learn by experimenting, adjusting, and trusting your instincts. That's neither deviant nor dangerous.

The real issue isn't the desire—it's the silence and shame that surround it.

Myth #24—Sexual Words Are Gross, Vulgar, and Disrespectful

It's easy to think that sexual words are inherently crude or that using them is disrespectful. Some may seem to automatically cross the line—but context is everything. The truth is, some words that feel uncomfortable or even offensive in everyday life can feel incredibly hot when you're aroused. Our brains don't process sexual stimuli the same way when we're turned on. What might seem "too much" in a regular conversation can suddenly become a turn-on in the right moment.

The same applies to sexual activities themselves. Things we once dismissed as *"not for me"* can take on a whole different energy when our body and mind are in sync and open. (See Myth #25.)

But here's the flip side: Not everyone responds to language in the same way. A word you find sexy might make your partner cringe—and vice versa. That's why it's worth talking about, openly and free of shame.

I use a tool with couples that is a simple sexual language inventory (see page 90 or website for resource), where each partner indicates how they feel about various words. But there's a twist: They're also asked to imagine how they'd feel about those words *when turned on*. Because arousal shifts perception—this exercise often surprises people in the best way. The goal isn't to create the "right" list of words; it's to start a conversation. To discover what turns you on, what turns you off, and what might be worth revisiting in the right moment. It's not about policing language—it's about understanding each other's boundaries and desires more clearly. Because the real question isn't, "*Is this word bad?*" It's: "*How do we both feel about this word, and when?*"

That kind of honest, curious conversation isn't about rules—it's about discovery. When you take the time to explore what excites you, what doesn't, and what might surprise you at the right moment, you're not just learning new words; you're gathering "ingredients." The kind that can transform a simple "dish" into something bold and utterly unforgettable.

Myth #25—A Sexual Activity That One Perceives as Gross, Messy, or Weird When Not Being Sexual Can Be Perceived as the Opposite When Feeling Sexual

There are things that, in broad daylight, might make you turn up your nose—certain sexual positions, fantasies, or scenarios that seem too messy, too weird, or too excessive. And yet, in a state of arousal, those same things can feel deeply erotic.

It's not a contradiction; it's context.

When we're aroused, our brain shifts. We perceive touch, language, and even ideas through a different lens. What may seem off-limits or awkward in our everyday, task-oriented mindset can suddenly become exciting when arousal takes the wheel. That doesn't make us deviant. It makes us human.

When people try to split these parts of themselves into rigid boxes—"*This is who I am outside of sex, and this is who I'm supposed to become during sex*"—such compartmentalization leaves no room for curiosity and certainly no room for nuance.

Sexual dreams, private fantasies, or bodily curiosity often trigger guilt in people raised to believe that sexual thoughts are shameful—or worse, sinful. I've worked with adults who still carry deep shame from childhood—people who were humiliated for masturbating or caught exploring their bodies, then punished or made to feel ashamed. Such experiences don't just disappear; they distort the natural relationship we're meant to have with our own bodies and desires. Feeling shame around pleasure is like trying to enjoy dessert while someone shames you for the calories.

You are *allowed* to think about sex. You are *allowed* to be curious. And you are *allowed* to be surprised by what turns you on when you're in an aroused state.

Sexuality doesn't always follow logic. Sometimes it manifests in ways we didn't foresee—and that's okay. There's nothing wrong with a little mess, a little surprise, or a little "I didn't know I'd be into that." What matters isn't how tidy your fantasies are; it's how safe, consensual, and, yes, at times, how unexpected your experiences can be.

Myth #26—Everyone Has Hot Wedding Night Sex— and Even Hotter Sex on the Honeymoon

Cue the cinematic montage: champagne glasses, candlelight, silky sheets . . . and two newlyweds falling into bed, completely in sync, passionately undressing each other, culminating with fireworks right outside the window of the bridal suite.

But your actual wedding night may resemble sore feet, exhaustion, and the emotional crash that follows a fourteen-hour social event. It's natural to wonder: *Did we do it wrong?*

Wedding night sex is not a universal milestone. For many couples, it doesn't happen at all. That doesn't mean anything is wrong with the relationship—it just means you're human. You've just spent an entire day being photographed, hugged, toasted, and pulled in a dozen directions. It's not exactly the ideal setup for relaxed, connected intimacy. Expecting to have mind-blowing sex on your wedding night is like saying, "*Go run a marathon, then come home and host an after-party in your bedroom.*"

Maybe not.

The same goes for the honeymoon. It's not uncommon for couples to come to therapy and confess, a little sheepishly, "*We didn't even have sex on our honeymoon.*" Or, "*We only had sex once or twice on our honeymoon.*" They often spiral into questions like, "*What does that mean? Are we already in trouble?*"

The answer is: Not necessarily. Just because you've been handed the keys to the kitchen doesn't mean you should immediately start cooking five-star meals. Sometimes, the best dishes come later—when you've had time to ponder, taste, and truly get to know what you're working with.

Of course, if there's a disconnect or avoidance that keeps happening, it's worth exploring. But more often, the problem isn't the sex—it's the pressure. The *expectation* that a honeymoon must include wall-to-wall sex in every corner of the resort (the bed, the pool, the shower, the balcony . . .) can be unrealistic, especially when you're still adjusting to travel, stress, the let-down that sometimes follows an exciting and long-planned wedding, and the new dynamics of being a couple.

You *might* have amazing sex. And you might even have a lot of it. But if you don't? That doesn't mean your spark is suddenly gone. It just means you're normal.

Good sex doesn't follow a schedule. It thrives on connection and curiosity—not deadlines. So, if your wedding night ends with takeout in bed and someone falls asleep halfway through a kiss, that's still a love story. Just not the one with a slow-motion fade-out and a romantic soundtrack.

Myth #27—Your Love Language Doesn't Affect How You Feel Desired During Sex

There's a common belief that feeling loved emotionally and feeling desired sexually are two separate things. However, for most of us, they're deeply intertwined. If words of affirmation make you feel loved in daily life, then chances are you'll feel more desired in bed when your partner says something affirming about your body or your presence. If quality time is your go-to, being fully focused on during intimacy can make the whole experience feel richer and more connected. These are extensions of the same emotional blueprint.

Understanding what makes you feel seen and cared for outside of sex can inspire a recipe for what might make sex feel more intimate and satisfying. Love languages don't simply disappear when the lights go out—they flavor the entire dish. The more attuned you are to those flavors, the easier it is to create something deeply satisfying.

Myth #28—What You Fantasize About Is What You Actually Want

Not necessarily.

Fantasies can be confusing and even confronting—but that doesn't mean they reflect your true desires or values. Sometimes, a fantasy is less about what you want to *do* and more about how you want to *feel*. It might be about power, vulnerability, mystery, or freedom—not necessarily the exact scenario playing out in your mind.

Consider someone who feels a lack of control in their daily life—they might fantasize about being in a dominant role, not because they truly desire that in reality, but because the fantasy offers an emotional release. It's emotional contrast, not a literal wish list.

Many people feel distressed by their fantasies. They wonder, *What does this say about me?* However, fantasizing about something doesn't mean you truly want to act it out. It indicates that your mind is exploring. That's what human minds do.

Sometimes, our fantasies involve things we'd never want to pursue in real life, yet they still ignite something within us. That's not wrong; it's simply part of how sexual imagination operates. What matters most is approaching your fantasies with curiosity rather than shame, and recognizing that they don't define you. They're merely one way your mind explores the concepts of pleasure, control, and identity.

Myth #29—If You Wait Long Enough, Sex Will Be Even Better

People often believe that if they wait a long time to have sex—weeks, months, or even years—that when it finally happens, it'll be off-the-charts hot. Like they've been storing up all this desire in some secret vault and the release will be explosive.

But that's not usually how it works.

The longer you go without being sexual—either with yourself or with a partner—the more you may need to recalibrate. Hesitation, awkwardness, or even performance anxiety can arise. You might wonder, *Do they still want me?* Or, *Will this feel the same?* And even if you've had sex with this person dozens or hundreds of times before, a long pause can still make the first time back feel unfamiliar.

It's not about *not* wanting sex—it's about comfort and momentum. Think of it like cooking a dish you haven't made in a while. You might remember the general steps, but you still need to reacquaint yourself with the ingredients, check the timing, and find the rhythm again. Sometimes you forget a step, and things can feel a little off. But with a little patience—and some creativity—it will come back to you.

Myth #30—If You Masturbate in a Relationship, You're Taking Something Away from Your Partner— or You Must Have a Problem

There's a persistent belief that self-pleasure somehow subtracts from your partnered sex life. That if you masturbate while in a relationship—especially on the same day you've had sex with your partner—it means something is wrong. *You're insatiable . . . and selfish.* Or worse, that you have a sexual addiction.

It simply isn't true.

Self-pleasure is a method through which people connect with themselves. It is personal and is unrelated to partner sex. It doesn't imply that you're rejecting your partner or avoiding intimacy; it simply means you're paying attention to your own body and pleasure, which is entirely your right. For some, it's more about relaxation, stress relief, or reconnecting with sensations rather than being "turned on." It serves as a way to recharge.

Partners may take it personally: "*We had sex yesterday, and now you're doing that?*" However, it doesn't mean something is lacking—it just signifies that you wanted solo time. It doesn't have to replace anything—or anyone.

Ultimately, pleasure isn't a zero-sum game. You can enjoy your own company while still deeply appreciating sex with your partner; one doesn't negate the other. Therefore, masturbation doesn't imply that you are dissatisfied with your partner or that something needs fixing.

What it means is that, when it comes to pleasure, nothing is off the table.

Chapter 2

The Flavor of Feminine Energy

"Sex is something you do;
sexuality is something you are."
~ Anna Freud

Feminine energy is sexuality embodied. It isn't defined by the superficial such as what you wear, how you speak, or how often you smile. It's more about the depth of your connection to yourself—your instincts, sensuality, creativity, and your ability to embody both strength and softness. It's not a performance or a facade. It's a presence, a way of being.

Many women, especially those who have devoted their lives to excelling in roles that demand ambition, structure, or leadership—such as running a business, raising a family, or managing everything from schedules to emergencies—may find embracing feminine energy somewhat unfamiliar. It could even feel unsafe. You might ask yourself: *How can I be powerful and soft? How can I be competent and sensual? How do I shift from steering the bus to letting someone else take the wheel—without losing myself?*

These are questions I often hear in my therapy office, and the confusion is clear. Our culture has long served up mixed messages: *Be successful, but don't be intimidating. Be sexy, but not too sexual. Be nurturing, but not needy. Be in control, but know when to surrender.* It's no wonder that many of us feel like we're constantly switching hats—or, worse, wearing all of them at once.

Feminine energy isn't about eliminating your strength, intellect, or drive; it's about integrating all aspects of yourself. Think of it as a beautiful, layered recipe. You don't need to abandon structure to enjoy the flow—there is beauty in improvisation. Remember that the most satisfying flavors often arise from contrast, like a hit of heat with a touch of sweet.

Sexually, this manifests in various ways. You might be someone who desires to be held, adored, and worshipped a little—all while feeling fierce and confident in the bedroom. You may wish to let go and feel cared for without sacrificing your voice or your power. And that's not weakness—it's clarity. That's understanding what you need to feel safe enough to open up, explore, and receive. That's emboldened feminine energy.

The invitation here isn't to perform a version of femininity you've seen in movies or magazines. It's to remain curious. Ask yourself: *What makes me feel feminine? What connects me to my body? What feels good, not because someone told me it should, but because it genuinely nourishes me?*

Maybe it's dancing in the kitchen or sinking into a hot bath with no plans afterward. There's no right way to be feminine—only your way. When you start showing up for yourself in that way, everything—including your sex life—begins to shift. You stop hustling to perform and start allowing yourself to feel. To receive. To be seen, not just as capable, but as human, whole, and worthy.

"Feminine energy" is one of those phrases that can feel either wildly inspiring or utterly confusing, depending on your day and your relationship with the term *feminine.*

In therapy, this confusion often arises. Women frequently share feelings such as, "*I'm powerful and ambitious at work, but I still want to feel soft and wanted in bed.*" Or, "*I've got so many responsibilities, I don't even know what being feminine means anymore.*" Or, "*I am capable and do most things myself without the help of anyone else, including a man, but then I am seen as not wanting to be supported or cared for.*"

And no wonder. The word *feminine* has been packaged and sold in countless ways—fragile, flirty, domestic, desirable, subservient, intuitive, mysterious, mystical. Depending on whom you ask, feminine energy is either a superpower or a liability.

However, if we approach it with curiosity rather than criticism, we discover that feminine energy isn't one-dimensional. It varies depending on our life stages, hormones, energy, and context—and, most importantly, how we personally define it. For some women, it represents sensuality and flow or assertiveness, capacity to care for many areas of life, and internal strength. For others, it signifies deep connection, slowness, or softness. And for many, it isn't even a fixed concept; it's a *state*—something you navigate in and out of like an internal rhythm, influenced by how safe, seen, and cared for you feel.

The challenge is that we often learn how to *lead, provide, plan,* and *protect*—all important skills. However, nobody teaches us how to be vulnerable and feel safe without feeling weak, or how to desire something profoundly and still feel worthy of receiving it. We are taught to care for others, but not always to claim the kind of care *we* want—especially in sexual relationships.

Of course, this shows up in the bedroom. Sometimes we lead there as well—not because we always want to, but because it's the role we are used to playing. But what if you don't *want* to be the director of the sexual experience all the time? What if, for once, you'd like to simply be cared for? Desired? Even doted on?

You're allowed to want that. You're allowed to want *both*— the leadership and the letting go.

Sometimes, the clearest path forward is to pause and stir the pot. Take a moment to check what's bubbling beneath the surface. The following questions aren't meant to judge— they're intended to invite a deeper kind of curiosity.

Questions to Reflect On to Understand Your Beliefs About Sex

When it comes to enjoying sex, what do you tell yourself?

____

____

____

Do you struggle to tell your partner what you want?

____

____

____

What are you afraid will happen if you do?

____

____

____

What (or whom) do you feel responsible for?

How does this sense of responsibility show up for you physically? How do you feel it in your body (scan your body)?

What does it feel like, emotionally, to have these responsibilities?

How did you come to have these responsibilities?

What else do you worry about when it comes to sex?

What do you tell yourself about yourself when you feel these concerns?

How do you believe others will perceive you when you pursue a desire?

What do you fear will happen, if you pursue a desire?

____

____

____

What are the benefits of avoiding or denying a sexual desire?

____

____

____

Were there any "aha" moments as you reflected on your answers?

____

____

____

The Seasons of Us: Maiden, Mother, Maga, Crone

We don't live in a straight line—especially not as women. We live in seasons and cycles. Like a well-loved recipe that changes slightly each time we make it, our bodies, desires, and energies shift with age and experience. There's no expiration date on sensuality; there's only the evolving rhythm of how we express it.

The **Maiden** phase—typically from girlhood to the mid-twenties—is a time when curiosity flourishes. It's a period of firsts: first sensations, first love, first heartbreak, and first taste of independence. This is when we begin to recognize what brings us joy (and what doesn't), as we explore pleasure with the excitement of someone tasting something for the first time. It's rarely organized, can be a bit awkward, but is filled with potential.

Then comes the **Mother** phase—not defined solely by whether you've given birth, but by a shift in energy toward nurturing, creation, and care. This can include parenting as well as birthing businesses, relationships, art, or communities. It's a time when sexual identity can feel overshadowed by responsibility. Bodies change. Roles expand. Intimacy sometimes gets pushed to the margins. Yet, within the fullness of this phase is a deepened capacity for sensuality—when we allow ourselves to reclaim it.

Maga represents the wise, wild middle. This stage has often been overlooked in traditional teachings, hidden between motherhood and menopause. Nonetheless, it deserves its own place at the table. The Maga years (roughly mid-thirties through late sixties) are complex and enriching. Many of us are building careers, raising children, maintaining homes, or nurturing dreams that took root in our younger years. There's a growing awareness of what we *don't* want, which creates space for more of what we *do* want. In this phase, sex often shifts from performance to depth. It's about connection, confidence, and claiming what we need—without apology.

Finally, there's the **Crone** stage—usually beginning around age seventy and extending into the next phase of life. The word *crone* has often been misused and given a harsh connotation, when, in fact, it's meant to honor wisdom. This time is for reflection, slow pace, and yes—pleasure, too. Women in this stage often talk about sex differently, with less urgency and more intimacy. There are fewer shoulds and more presence. It's the simmer, not the sizzle, that fulfills us in this stage of life.

Each phase brings its own flavor. None is better than another, and none disqualifies you from being sensual, sexual, or deeply connected to your body. You don't age *out* of sexual vitality; you evolve *into* new ways of experiencing it.

Feminine energy can shift throughout the seasons of a woman's life, too. What you crave, how you want to be touched, and how you desire to be seen—these aspects evolve. From the youthful curiosity of the Maiden to the expansive creativity of the Mother, and to the wise and fiery confidence of the Maga and Crone years, there's no single way to be "feminine." There's only what feels true for you at any given moment.

No matter where you are, you are not behind. It's not too late. You are simply in the season you're meant to be in.

Reflection: Where Are You in the Seasons of You?

These archetypal stages—Maiden, Mother, Maga, Crone—aren't rigid categories; they aren't solely defined by age. Instead, they overlap and loop back. You may embody a bit of each at any given time.

Take a moment to reflect on these questions, without judgment:

Which phase do you feel most connected to right now?
- Are you in a time of discovery and experimentation (Maiden)?
- A time of nurturing, creating, or giving to others (Mother)?
- A time of reclaiming space, speaking your truth, or refusing to settle (Maga)?
- A time of slowing down, holding wisdom, or seeking peace (Crone)?

Are there aspects of another phase whispering for your attention?

- Maybe you're in Maga mode, but your inner Maiden is craving play.
- Maybe you're a Crone with a fierce desire to create something new—channeling a bit of Mother.

How does your sexuality show up in this phase of your life?
- Are there new preferences, pleasures, or challenges you're noticing?
- Are there parts of your sexual self you've set aside—and might be ready to welcome back?

What do you need more of in this season?
- Permission? Rest? Curiosity? Celebration?

This reflection isn't about confining yourself. It's about observing the natural rhythm of your life and recognizing that your sexuality can always evolve, quieten, or ignite into something new.

• • • •

Feminine energy evolves as we change. Sometimes it is characterized by curiosity and discovery, marked by responsibility and creation, or it represents a time of authentically owning our true presence. Interestingly, the stage called Maga, often occurring post-menopause, is when many women report that the best sex of their lives begins. If you're wondering why, it's because they've stopped trying to prove anything. They're done tolerating what doesn't serve them, and they finally feel entitled to pleasure, softness, and being seen.

Some women refer to it as their "F-you" phase.

Others just call it *freedom*.

So, yes, you can be both powerful and soft, sensual and strong, grounded and exploratory. There is no *one* way to embody femininity; there is only the version that feels like *you*.

And if you're not sure what that is yet, that's okay, too. Start with curiosity. Ask: *What makes me feel feminine? What does that even mean to me?* Think of it as tasting your way through a new recipe—one you can tweak, spice up, or simplify based on what you're craving and who you're becoming. Because this isn't about fitting into someone else's mold.

The Seasons of Feminine Energy

As a sex therapist, I often find that my work circles back to one profound truth: Feminine energy isn't a fixed thing to be mastered—it's a constantly changing rhythm to be lived. Some women come into my office trying to reconnect with a spark they once knew. Others are just discovering it for the first time. Wherever they are on their journey, the path forward is always about integration—learning that *sex is something you do, but sexuality is something you are.*

What follows are glimpses into three women's stories, each passing through a different phase of her feminine life cycle— the Maiden, the Mother, and the Maga. These are not rigid roles but evolving seasons of the same landscape. Each woman learned to see herself more clearly, and in doing so, to live more fully in her own skin, thereby transforming her perception of herself, her life, and her personal self-care.

The Maiden: Discovering Joy and Curiosity

Carrie visited me in her mid-twenties—bright and expressive, yet quietly uncertain about who she truly was beneath all the expectations. Like many women in the Maiden phase, she had absorbed countless messages about how femininity "should" look: soft but not weak, sensual but not too much, confident but still agreeable.

Our work turned toward peeling back those layers of performance. Carrie started to ask herself questions she'd never been encouraged to ask: *What feels alive in me? What feels true?*

She started dancing again—sometimes alone, barefoot in her apartment, sometimes at classes just for the joy of movement. She painted, took herself on dates, and slowly began to understand that femininity wasn't something to earn approval for. It was something to inhabit. As she let go of performing desire, she began to *feel* desire—playful, curious, and entirely her own.

The Mother: Balancing Nurture and Self-Care

Rebecca, a client in her thirties, was navigating the Mother phase, balancing her career with family responsibilities. She felt her feminine energy was overshadowed by the demands of caring for others. Her nurturing energy was plentiful, but it all flowed outward—toward her family, colleagues, and community. Little remained for herself.

Together, we explored the idea that feminine energy doesn't vanish under responsibility—it simply gets buried. She didn't need to become someone new; she needed to create space for the woman who had been waiting beneath the lists and deadlines.

Rebecca began with small acts of reclamation: taking leisurely baths and setting boundaries that allowed her to practice self-care. This change improved both her personal well-being and her intimate relationships, as she learned to receive care and love without guilt. Over time, she noticed how tending to her own pleasure softened the edges of her fatigue. Her relationships also evolved. When she allowed herself to receive care instead of only giving it, intimacy deepened.

She learned that caring for herself isn't the opposite of loving others; it's the foundation of it.

The Maga: Reclaiming Space and Sexual Vitality

Linda began therapy in her late forties, just beginning to sense the power of the Maga—the midlife woman who has nothing left to prove. Still, she found herself caught up in old stories: that desire diminishes with age, and that her worth was tethered to who she used to be.

Our work centered on helping her let go of those narratives. The more she did, the more she began to notice a quieter, more grounded sensuality awakening within her. She started asserting what she wanted—in life and in bed—without apology.

For Linda, this phase was less about discovery and more about reclamation. She realized that her sexuality didn't need to appear youthful to be vibrant. It could be slower, deeper, and wildly confident. She started to see her body as an ally, not just a reminder of time passing.

In that acceptance, pleasure found her again—steady, knowing, radiant.

Integration: A Living Tapestry

Each of these women—Maiden, Mother, Maga—revealed a truth about feminine energy: It is not linear and never stops evolving. These archetypes are simply mirrors that reflect the facets of womanhood present within all of us at once.

Through therapy, these women didn't just reconnect with their sexuality—they learned to embody it fully. They discovered that feminine energy isn't about fitting into a construct; it's about giving yourself permission to thrive.

Your femininity is yours to define. It shifts with the tides of your life, with each season of becoming. And when you stop trying to control it, you might just discover that it was never lost—it was only waiting for you to come home.

Wherever you find yourself—whether in the thrill of discovery, the act of giving, the fire of reclaiming, or the calm of knowing—this is your season, and it's worthy of your presence. You don't need to rush to the next phase or apologize for the one you're currently experiencing. Feminine energy is a quiet, powerful knowing that flows through you, regardless of the stage you're in. Keep listening . . . exploring . . . asking. Your unfolding is more than enough.

Chapter 3

Pleasure On Purpose

Think of this chapter as an invitation to pause and take stock—like cleaning out the pantry to keep what's fresh—and tucking away a few surprises in the back. It's an opportunity to ask: What's expired? What's no longer useful? What's still delicious? What needs a few tweaks? Whether referring to attitudes, routines, relationships, or beliefs, this is about creating space for what nourishes you now.

At the heart of pleasure—especially sexual pleasure—is intentionality. That might mean starting anew with yourself or within a relationship, consciously building a foundation based not on assumptions but on shared curiosity and communication. It's about making a choice, not settling, and having conversations instead of crossing your fingers and hoping things will go well. Reconnecting not just with each other, but with your erotic self.

When couples take the time to understand their patterns—what works and what doesn't—they can begin to co-create something new. A sexual relationship can shift as life shifts. When you consider everything from energy levels and body image to past experiences, it becomes clear: Pleasure doesn't just happen. It's shaped, invited, and, yes, planned.

Most people fall into patterns without realizing it. We rarely pause to ask ourselves or each other if we're satisfied—because doing so can feel awkward or risky. We repeat routines, default to familiar dynamics, and forget to ask the simplest questions: *Is this working? Do I actually like this?* Or even, *How did we get here?* If we consider broaching the subject, we wonder, *Will it seem like criticism? Will they think I'm unhappy?*

But here's the thing: It's not about criticism. It's about responsibility. Sex is part of your life—and just like you'd reflect on your career after a significant life change, or reassess your fitness goals after having kids, you can check in on your sex life as your relationship, body, and life circumstances evolve.

That's what "pleasure on purpose" really means. It's not a rigid to-do list—it's a process of reflection and imagination. What is your sex life like now? What has it been like before? What do you want it to become? This is where you take inventory—not with judgment, but with openness. Think of it as rewriting the recipe to better suit your current tastes. Maybe your palate has changed. Maybe your partner's has, too. This reflection is a powerful tool that can empower you to shape your sexual relationship.

You don't need all the answers. Start with questions. Try brainstorming together. Toss around ideas. What did you enjoy last time? What's something you've been curious about? What's one thing you'd like more of—or less of? This open communication can help you feel more connected and understood in your sexual relationship.

Then visualize what that could look like. Play it out in your mind. Try something new, like a different position or a new location. Adjust as needed. Keep the conversation going. You might find yourself returning to old favorites, such as a particular type of foreplay, or discovering something new that really clicks, like a new role-playing scenario. The goal isn't perfection—it's attention.

This kind of planning also asks you to look at how you feel, not just about sex, but about yourself. Ask: *What do I want? What do I like? Do I feel free in my body, or am I going through the motions? How do I think about who I am when I'm being sexual? Do I feel safe? Do I feel seen?*

Because sex doesn't exist in a vacuum. The stories we've heard—whether from parents, peers, movies, or books—shape our beliefs. The warnings about pregnancy or STIs, the scripts we've inherited about what's "normal," or what's "too much," all of that comes into the bedroom whether we realize it or not. And sometimes, our fears and self-doubt come from someone else's story, not our own.

The good news? You can change the narrative. You can do a complete renovation—or just repaint the walls. You don't need to leave your partner, start over, have an affair, or blow up your life to experience newness or growth. Sometimes, the freshest start comes from reimagining what you already have.

Even if things have been tense—bickering, distance, disconnection—it's still possible to begin again. That might mean letting go of grudges, forgiving past missteps, or simply making space for something different. You don't have to forget—but you don't have to stay stuck either.

Remember, a fresh start is always on the table, and it offers a sense of hope and possibility for your future sexual relationship.

Making a Plan

When I sit down with couples, one of the most powerful tools I use is what I call a *sexual timeline*. It's a simple idea, really—just a look back at how intimacy has evolved in the relationship. What was sex like when you first met? What made it playful, electric, or meaningful? And how has it changed since then? What feels different now—what's missing that once seemed easy? What parts of your connection no longer fit or serve you? And, perhaps most importantly, what do you long to bring back into the relationship?

Reflecting on these questions isn't about dwelling on what's lost, but about remembering what's been built together. Revisiting your shared history can be a beautiful reminder of your bond—a spark of encouragement to nurture the love, curiosity, and attention that keep a relationship alive.

Creating this timeline together helps couples rediscover forgotten desires or moments of connection that may have been buried beneath the day-to-day pressures of life. Sometimes it's something small—a way of looking at each other, a lingering touch before leaving for work, a private joke whispered across the dinner table. These moments aren't always explicitly sexual, but they are intimately charged and lay the foundation for desire.

Once you start mapping it out, you may begin to notice patterns: times when sex felt easy and joyful, and times when it felt like effort or obligation. You might observe that certain seasons of life came with more stress or disconnection, while others brought more warmth or freedom. This reflective process isn't about blame—it's about understanding your own sexual story and seeing how it has shaped where you are now.

From this foundation, we move toward co-creating a new vision. This isn't about setting rigid goals or forcing new behaviors. It's about *imagining together.* What would it look like to feel more connected? What would be exciting to try, or comforting to return to? What have you been doing out of habit, and what new ideas are you eager to explore?

Visualization can be a powerful way to begin. Close your eyes and imagine the intimate experience you desire—how it starts, how you feel, what is said or done. Pay attention to the atmosphere. Is there music? Is there laughter? Is it slow and sensual, or playful and spontaneous? This type of mental rehearsal helps bring your desires into focus. It primes your brain and body to recognize opportunities for pleasure that you might otherwise overlook.

I often begin with something tangible, like a recent sexual experience. I'll ask a couple to walk me through it—not just what occurred during sex, but what happened around it. What was the mood of the day? Did someone prepare dinner or share a funny story? Was there tension, exhaustion—or warmth—in the air?

We trace the arc together. What sparked the connection? What created momentum? What stalled it? These "before moments" matter more than most people realize. They shape the tone and emotional safety of what follows. They also offer clues about what truly matters to each partner in feeling open, relaxed, and receptive to pleasure.

Next, we delve into the details. What felt good? What wasn't so great? What do you wish had gone differently? This is where honest, nonjudgmental conversation becomes essential. It's not just about what went "right" or "wrong." It's about fine-tuning the shared experience—adjusting pressure, pacing, and emotional tone. You're not fixing a broken machine. You're evolving a living, breathing relationship.

And don't underestimate the value of checking your assumptions. I've seen many situations where one partner thought, *They love it when I do that*, only to find out their partner had just been going along with it out of habit or politeness. These moments of recalibration aren't failures—they're openings. They create space for a truer connection and deeper mutual satisfaction.

To support this process, I sometimes use personalized questionnaires with my clients, and I've included one at the end of this chapter. These tools encourage each individual to explore their preferences, boundaries, and curiosities—everything from their favorite types of touch to fantasies they've never shared. Each person completes the questions independently at first, and then we compare responses to identify overlaps, discover new possibilities, and pinpoint areas for conversation.

Think of it like curating a celebratory dinner together. You're not committing to cook every dish, but you're gaining a clearer sense of what sounds appealing, what might need a little spicing up, and what's better left off the menu. It eliminates guesswork and eases pressure. Often, it also creates a sense of excitement—like flipping through a new cookbook and discovering a recipe you can't wait to try.

Of course, all of this takes place within the realm of *sensation*. One of the most overlooked aspects of sexual pleasure is our experience of touch, sound, temperature, smell, and even light. Our sensory preferences and sensitivities are as unique as our fingerprints, and understanding them can change how we engage in bed—and in life.

Consider touch, for example. One partner reaches out while the other pulls back. The instinctive assumption is rejection. However, it's often not that at all. It could simply be that the touch was too sudden, too firm, or unexpected. Some people need a moment to orient themselves and settle into the sensation. Their nervous system requires time to shift from neutral to receptive. That pause isn't a no—it's a "not yet."

Similarly, sounds that may be comforting or arousing to one person might be distracting or overwhelming to another. Lighting that feels cozy to one partner might seem too dim or too bright to the other. Even scents can trigger memories or subtly yet significantly impact emotional states. None of this is trivial—it's all data. It's information that helps you create an experience that feels inviting and supportive, not jarring or depleting.

Sometimes, these sensory preferences have been pathologized. People are told they're "too sensitive" or "too particular," when, in fact, they're simply attuned to their own systems. Learning to honor those needs—and communicate them—can reduce unnecessary conflict and make the overall experience feel safer and more enjoyable.

Ultimately, this isn't about becoming perfect lovers. It's about becoming *attuned.* Pleasure isn't a one-size-fits-all experience; it's a collaborative unfolding. The more information you have—about your timeline, your desires, and your sensory world—the better equipped you are to create something satisfying, meaningful, and real.

• • • •

I recall a client named Julia whose story beautifully illustrates the evolution of pleasure and connection. She approached me seeking to understand what had shifted in her intimate life—why pleasure seemed just beyond her grasp, and how she might intentionally rediscover it. Together, we started by exploring her perceptions of desire and satisfaction, identifying what still felt vibrant and what had become distant.

I shared an image that resonated with her: pleasure as a pantry that sometimes needs refreshing, or a recipe ready for a new twist. You keep the flavors that still delight you, clear out what's gone stale, and play with fresh ingredients. That metaphor became our framework—a gentle invitation to curiosity and reinvention.

Julia entered our sessions with a mix of curiosity and hesitation. I encouraged her to look not only at her sexual experiences but also at how she connected with her partner—where comfort once existed, and where silence had taken its place. As she reflected, she began to notice how often she moved through intimacy on autopilot, repeating patterns that no longer matched what she genuinely wanted.

The turning point happened when she realized that pleasure isn't just something that happens—it's something we participate in. To help her see this more clearly, we developed the sexual timeline of her relationship, marking moments that shaped her understanding of intimacy. Reflecting on early memories brought back the joy and spontaneity that had once come easily.

From there, she started asking new questions—gentle, honest ones: *What do I want now? What do we enjoy together?*

What once felt uncomfortable began to feel freeing. Conversations that used to feel risky became gateways to closeness and laughter.

As Julia became more comfortable expressing her needs, she also reconnected with her body's subtle cues—the sensations that made her feel alive. She stopped just performing and began truly experiencing. Through this, she and her partner discovered that intimacy didn't have to be perfectly planned; it only needed attention and willingness.

By the end of our work, Julia's perspective had shifted. She no longer saw sex as a chore but as a vital part of her relationship—something meant to grow, evolve, and surprise. This was her invitation to rewrite the "recipe" of her sexual life, tailoring it to her changing palate. It taught her to embrace her sexuality openly, inviting both herself and her partner to reshape their intimate life with intention, curiosity, and endless possibilities—a testament to the transformative power of purpose in nurturing fulfilling sexual connections.

Her story became a reminder that pleasure, like love itself, flourishes when tended with curiosity and care.

Pleasure Is Also a Practice

Like cooking, dancing, or learning an instrument, sexual pleasure deepens with practice. This isn't about performance; it's about familiarity, rhythm, and responsiveness. We need to get to know our bodies and then revisit that understanding repeatedly, because what delights us can change with mood, context, age, and phases of life.

What feels good one week may feel different the next. Something that once worked might lose its magic, and something that never clicked before could suddenly come alive. The only way to find out is to *stay curious*—and keep practicing.

Pleasure isn't a onetime discovery; it's a living, evolving experience. While orgasm may be one destination, it's certainly not the only one. You can absolutely have fulfilling, nourishing, toe-tingling sex without climax. That said, if orgasm is part of what you're hoping to explore more deeply, practice is the way to get there.

You might even stumble into a great orgasm by surprise, only to find yourself wondering: *Wait—what just happened? That's* a beautiful moment to pause and reflect: *What was I thinking about? How was I touched? What did my body feel like before, during, and after?*

That type of reflection is the difference between merely hoping something works and truly understanding *how* it works *for you.*

Intentionality is the secret ingredient. It doesn't mean being serious all the time. Purposeful practice creates space for more spontaneity, more play, and more joy. Just like learning a sport, you initially focus on the fundamentals, but eventually, you find flow. You play and invent—and sometimes you might even surprise yourself.

That's when sex becomes not just something you *do,* but something you *live into.*

From Reflection to Action

So, what does it truly mean to act on this fresh start?

It begins with awareness—and continues with curiosity. The more you can name your desires, your longings, and your uncertainties, the more direction you provide for your exploration. This applies to solo self-discovery as much as it does to shared intimacy. By allowing yourself to engage in dialogue—with your body, your thoughts, your fantasies, and your partner—you cultivate a relationship with pleasure that is both informed and dynamic.

Start with something small. Maybe it's a new question: "What if we slowed everything down?" or "What if we started without any expectations?" Perhaps it's an experiment with a different kind of touch, a new setting, or even just using your words more freely: "I'm feeling really connected to you right now," or "I loved it when you kissed my back the other night."

Language can be erotic; it can also be grounding. When we allow ourselves to talk about sex—intentionally, not performatively—we bring our whole selves into the experience, closing the gap between what we feel and what we express.

And if talking feels difficult? That's okay, too. That's part of the practice. Like learning a new language, it can take time to become fluent in expressing your needs, curiosities, and boundaries. That's why it helps to have tools—whether it's a worksheet, a guided meditation, or even just a few simple prompts to start the conversation.

Here's one to try: "Tell me something you'd like us to do more of." Or, "What's something we haven't tried yet that you've thought about?" These aren't high-stakes interrogations. They're invitations. Think of them as appetizers—small bites that whet the appetite for deeper connection.

And remember, you don't have to tackle it all at once. There's no rush. The journey toward more fulfilling, intentional sex is a long table full of options. You can start with one course. You can savor what works and set aside what doesn't. This is about pacing, preference, and practice.

Reflection-Guided Meditation

Introduction

This guided meditation is designed to help you relax, connect with your inner self, and attune to your desires, sensations, and pleasure. It invites you to explore a deep awareness of your body and breath, offering a space for reflection on past and current intimate experiences, and supports you in setting your intentions for the future.

Find a comfortable, quiet place to sit or lie down and gently close your eyes.

Begin by taking a deep breath in through your nose, feeling your chest and abdomen expand.

Hold your breath for a moment, and then slowly release through your mouth, noticing the sensation as the air leaves your body.

As you continue to breathe deeply and evenly, bring your focus to each part of your body, imagining relaxation and, as you exhale, release any tension that you may be holding.

Focus on the gentle rise and fall of your chest with each breath.

Feel your heart space open and expand, welcoming love and connection.

Now visualize a warm, glowing light at the center of your being.

This light represents your true essence and desires. Let it expand with each breath, filling your entire body with warmth, lightness, and serenity.

Gently bring to mind some of your past intimate and sexual experiences.

Observe them without judgment, acknowledging each one as they arise.

Which experiences brought joy and fulfillment?

____

____

____

What lessons did they impart?

____

____

____

Are there elements you'd like to retain or transform?

____

____

____

Allow yourself to explore these reflections with compassion and curiosity, recognizing the growth and learning each experience has provided for you.

Now shift your focus to your present intimate and sexual life.

Which aspects align with your true self and desires?

____

____

____

How do these experiences resonate with your body and emotions?

____

____

____

Are there experiences that stand out as positive or challenging?

____

____

____

Embrace your current experiences with gratitude and understanding, acknowledging their role in your ongoing journey.

Now direct your attention to your desires, sensations, and pleasure.

Allow yourself to be fully present with these feelings.

What do you truly desire in your intimate connections?

____

____

____

How do various sensations contribute to your pleasure?

____

____

____

In what ways can you honor and enhance your pleasure?

____

____

____

As you breathe, imagine each sensation as a wave, guiding you toward authenticity and fulfillment.

Allow these feelings to help you tune in more deeply to your true wants and needs.

Visualize what fulfilling, joyful connections would look and feel like to you.

Which elements are essential for your ideal experiences?

____

____

____

How can you nurture these aspects going forward?

____

____

____

What, if anything, should you release to create space for growth?

____

____

____

Now take a moment to set a gentle intention for yourself.

Take another deep breath in and begin to bring your awareness back to the present moment, feeling each breath moving in and out of your body and feeling the connection to your body.

Begin to wiggle your fingers and toes, gently stretching, and then, when you're ready, begin to open your eyes.

Affirmations

Repeat to yourself: "I am attuned to my body, desires, and sensations. I welcome pleasure and joy into my life with gratitude and openness."

Questionnaire

Couples Sexual Questions

Responses

Yes, sounds fun!

Maybe, if my partner was interested.

No, I don't have any interest in this.

Part One

How often would you like to have sex (all forms of sexual activity)?

Do you enjoy oral sex?

____

____

____

Do you enjoy kissing?

____

____

____

Do you enjoy manual stimulation?

Do you enjoy anal play or penetration?

Would you be interested in mutual masturbation (masturbation while with each other)?

Would you like to initiate sex more often?

Would you like your partner to initiate sex more often?

Would you like to have morning sex?

Would you like to have sex in the middle of the night?

Would you like to have longer teasing and foreplay?

____

____

____

Would you like to give or receive a sensual massage?

____

What are three things that you find to be romantic?

    1. _______________________________

    2. _______________________________

    3. _______________________________

What are three things that make you feel interested (desire) in being sexual?

    1. _______________________________

    2. _______________________________

    3. _______________________________

What are three things that make you feel turned on (arousal)?

    1. _______________________________

    2. _______________________________

    3. _______________________________

Would you like to watch porn with your partner?

____

____

____

Would you like to role-play in costumes?

____

____

____

Would you like to listen to music while having sex? If so, what kind (romantic, classical, rock, rap, heavy metal, or something else)?

____

____

Are there sexual positions that you prefer?

____

____

Are there sexual positions that you would like to try again?

____

____

Are there sexual positions that you are interested in trying, but have not tried before?

____

____

What kind of fantasies do you have?

____

____

Do you enjoy them?

____

____

Would you like to share any of them with your partner?

____

____

Would you like to use toys during sex?

If so, what kind (dildos, vibrators, cock ring—vibrating/non-vibrating)?

Chapter 4

Tending the Temple

When Amelia first came to see me, she was running on empty. A gentle, thoughtful woman in her late thirties, she had spent years attending to everyone else's needs and quietly putting her own last. Pleasure felt distant. Rest felt like a reward she hadn't earned.

We began with a reframe: What if self-care wasn't indulgent, but essential? Through assessing where she was directing her energy and focusing on what mattered most to her, she began to see her needs as valid and worthy of attention. I introduced her to the concept of the cascade effect—how even a small act of care, done intentionally, could shift the whole day. Amelia started carving out fifteen minutes just for herself. No goals or multitasking—simply some space.

From there, we built her "pleasure toolbox"—textures, sounds, and rituals that helped her feel grounded and alive. She began to explore her body again, slowly and on her own terms. At first, it felt unfamiliar. Then, it became empowering. Her self-awareness grew, and so did her conversations around intimacy.

Perhaps the most significant shift was not in her routine but in her mindset. She stopped saying "I have to" and started saying "I get to." Rest became something she allowed herself, not something she postponed for later. And in that stillness, she remembered that her sensuality wasn't something to chase —it was something that had always belonged to her.

• • • •

Self-care has become one of those phrases we toss around like confetti—well-intentioned but, when overused, it can become annoying. It's everywhere—on mugs, pinned to vision boards, and whispered in yoga classes—but what does it truly mean in daily life? Self-care, at its core, involves caring for yourself in ways that are personal, genuinely nurturing, and rejuvenating.

Self-care is not a spa day. It's not merely drinking green juice or booking a massage, though those can be lovely and nourishing things. It's about tending to your life like you would a garden. It involves showing up, checking in, noticing what needs watering, what needs pruning, and what's blooming beautifully. It's the daily, sometimes challenging, often peaceful act of observing and listening, then responding with compassion.

When life gets stressful—and for most of us, that's often the case—self-care helps bring us back to center. It's not indulgent or selfish, but it definitely takes practice. It builds our resilience and is how we protect our well-being and capacity for joy. It doesn't happen by accident; it requires intention and a little planning.

The Cascade Effect

Self-care doesn't always seem life-changing or dramatic in the moment. Sometimes it's as simple as going to bed half an hour earlier, saying no to something you don't want to do, and choosing water over coffee. Yet, these small acts create a ripple effect. When we start to treat ourselves like someone worth caring for, we change how we move through the world. There's a cascade effect. One act of care leads to another. We begin to notice and ultimately make different choices. We start to imagine that life could feel . . . better. Maybe we deserve to feel good, not someday, but today.

This tending of the temple requires honest introspection. *Why do I feel depleted? What have I been avoiding? What would it mean to be gentle with myself, not just when things are going well, but especially when they aren't?*

Self-care isn't about becoming a different person. It's about coming home to yourself.

Not Selfish, Just Self-Compassion

Reminder: Self-care and selfishness are not synonymous. One is about sustenance; the other is about exclusion. Taking care of yourself doesn't mean ignoring others—it's about being able to support them without losing yourself in the process by overextending and overaccommodating. No one else is responsible for how you inhabit your body, mind, or emotional landscape. That's your domain. The more you nurture it with love, the more stable and joyful everything else becomes. Because when your inner world is rooted in self-love, you stop needing as much external validation. You become your own reference point. From that place, you begin to make choices that align with your values, rather than merely trying to avoid rejection or seeking approval. You begin by saying, "This feels right for me," and trusting that voice.

Teaching Others How to Treat You

Here's something we weren't taught in health class: You are always teaching people how to treat you. Every "yes," every "no," and every boundary (spoken or unspoken) sends a message. Over time, these signals create a pattern—an ecosystem of expectations. If you've been consistently overriding your own needs, people will assume that's what works for you. Not because they're trying to take advantage, but because that's what you've demonstrated to them.

If that touches a nerve, believe me, you are not alone. Most of us have spent years tuning out our own discomfort to keep the peace, be likable, or stay "easygoing." But self-care encourages us to reconnect with ourselves. It asks: *What do I want? What have I been tolerating that no longer feels right?* This is how we reclaim ourselves—physically, emotionally, and sexually. We don't need to override anyone else's needs. We just stop abandoning our own.

There is a quiet rebellion in self-care: You decide what's yours to keep and what you need to let go of. You hold the power to create a value system that aligns with your truth, not someone else's. And you don't have to do everything all at once. Begin with one belief—one old idea that says, "You can't," or "You shouldn't," or "That's not for people like you." Hold it up to the light. Ask: *Is this still true? Was it ever?*

From Surviving to Savoring

Many of us spend years—decades, even—living in survival mode. We hustle. We power through. We "get through the day." While that can be necessary at times, it isn't meant to be permanent. So what does it mean to transition from survival to sensuality?

Sensuality isn't a leap; it's a slow dance. Noticing, remembering . . . It's the difference between hurriedly wolfing down a meal and savoring the first bite of something warm and satisfying.

Creating moments of sensual awareness in your day is a way to begin reclaiming pleasure. Not just sexual pleasure—but everyday pleasure. The joy of soft fabric on your skin, a warm breeze, or the sound of beautiful music. These experiences are not frivolous; they're fuel. Explore what invites your sensuality to the surface, and welcome more of that into your life.

The Pleasure Toolbox

Taking this idea further, I often encourage people to consider creating a pleasure toolbox—whether literally or metaphorically. And no, I don't mean a pink box filled with glitter and vibrators (although, if that's your thing . . .). This is a collection of objects, practices, memories, and sensory cues that reconnect you with a sense of groundedness and desire—whether it's the desire to relax, to feel more comfortable in your skin, or to embrace sensuality.

Think of this as a way to sprinkle a bit more intentional pleasure into your day. The "contents" of your toolbox are entirely your own. It could be a favorite phrase on a sticky note that helps you reframe the moment, or a photo of your partner that evokes a tender memory. It might be something playful you're both looking forward to, or simply the scent of a specific lotion or fragrance that slows you down when you apply it, grounding you in your senses and inviting a pause. Using a journal to explore how each item in your metaphorical toolbox supports you may be helpful. Reflect on how each tool in your self-care toolbox makes you feel—and notice which ones nourish you and which might need a refresh. What's working? What has lost its spark?

These may seem like small acts, but they make a significant impact. They disrupt the stress-response cycle and create micro-moments of embodiment. During those moments, you reconnect with yourself. And it's not just about general self-care; this is also sexual self-care. When you choose something that helps you reconnect with your body, soothe your nervous system, or shift your energy into a more curious, receptive state, you are nurturing the roots of your erotic self.

Once you've filled your self-care toolbox with daily supports, you can begin adding layers of intentional sexual self-care. Consider how you prefer to initiate intimacy—or how you would like to be approached. Take the time to outline it—and make it playful. Compile a list in your journal of things you've always been curious about. I like to call this a sexual bucket list. If the word *bucket list* feels too bold or intimidating, think of it as a menu—a range of "maybe one day" possibilities. You don't have to try everything on the menu, but identifying the flavors you're curious about opens up space for surprise and permission.

Reframing the Day

I often suggest to clients that they try playing with the semantics we use to describe their daily tasks. Instead of "I have to," try "*I get to*" as a subtle but powerful way to look at things a little differently.

"I get to go home and rest."
"I get to take five minutes to stretch."
"I get to light a candle, read a book, and unwind."

You're not channeling Pollyanna—you're just allowing yourself to focus on what's possible. We all have stress and negativity in our lives. But by changing the language, you are *reclaiming the parts of your day that belong to you*. Your life is not just a checklist to get through; it's a place to inhabit, a body to feel at home in, and there's a rhythm for you to rediscover.

Even the anticipation of something nurturing can create a shift. Knowing that a moment of comfort or connection is waiting for you can soften the edges of a tough day. The more you embrace that anticipation, the more vivid those moments become.

Sacred Space

There is a frequently underestimated form of self-care—especially for women and, most notably, for caregivers—and that is solitude. Time spent alone in quiet, undisturbed solitude. Most of us live in a world of shared everything: shared bedrooms, bathrooms, workspaces, and calendars. And that's not necessarily a problem. Shared spaces can be deeply intimate and connective. However, we also need space that's solely ours—a place where no one asks us for anything, and where we're not performing, explaining, negotiating, or accommodating.

I advocate for this kind of sacred personal space with nearly every client. It doesn't have to be fancy; it could be a small room (some of my clients have used a walk-in closet!) or a nook with a soft blanket and a candle. What matters is that it's yours. And there's an agreement—spoken or unspoken—that when you're there, you are not to be disturbed, and you get to be off-duty.

When your nervous system realizes that no one will barge in, ask a question, or need you right this second, something magical happens: It begins to settle. There's a physiological response. You shift from alertness to ease. It's like the difference between always sleeping with one eye open and finally being able to exhale. Transitioning from bracing to softening is where your healing happens. Where you reconnect with yourself—not just as a role you play, but as a person with autonomy, needs, and desires—beautiful things can happen.

Once you've claimed your sacred space, you get to decide how to use it. You might meditate, journal, stretch, nap, read, or listen to music that transports you. You could engage in an art project like adult coloring books or knitting—something tactile that brings you into the moment. You might choose to masturbate—or simply stare out the window. There are no rules; the only requirement is that the space feels good to you and is protected. It should reflect your energy, not what anyone else thinks it should be. It doesn't have to be created with someone else in mind—it just needs to be yours.

Sometimes, I guide clients through a visualization to help them envision what this kind of space could look like. If you had a private, cozy corner just for you, what would it look like? What colors would be there? Would there be soft textures, twinkly lights, and stacks of books? Would it be near a window or tucked away from the world?

And then I ask: Do you have something like that already—and just haven't claimed it yet? Or is it time to create it? Often, people don't realize how much they crave this kind of space until they start to imagine it. Suddenly, the longing becomes clear. The lack transforms into something they can identify. The permission to create it becomes something they finally allow themselves.

Consider using the following guided meditation as inspiration to create a sacred space at home—a place where you can pause, breathe, and reconnect with yourself.

Guided Meditation: Creating Your Sacred Space

Start by getting comfortable, either sitting or lying down.

Close your eyes gently, and take a slow, deep breath in.

Pause for a moment, then exhale completely.

As you keep breathing deeply, relax and release any tension.

With each breath, notice yourself becoming more centered and calm.

Inhale tranquility and exhale any stress or distractions.

Now, imagine a sanctuary inside your home or yard, a space that is entirely your own.

Picture yourself standing at the entrance to this personal retreat.

Visualize it as a place where you are uninterrupted and at peace.

As you step inside, take a moment to observe your surroundings.

What part of your home or yard have you chosen for this sacred space?

Is it a cozy corner of a room, a sunlit veranda, or a quiet nook in your garden?

Begin to personalize this space with elements that bring you joy and reflect your essence.

Picture soft, comfortable seating, perhaps a plush chair or hammock, where you can easily relax.

Consider the colors that adorn your space—shades that soothe or invigorate.

Imagine bringing in decorations that speak to your heart.

Maybe there's a small altar with meaningful objects, plants that breathe life and serenity, or artwork that inspires and uplifts you.

Consider the sounds you wish to include.

Perhaps a gentle breeze rustles leaves in your yard; maybe the soft trickle of a fountain or the quiet hum of nature surrounds you.

Or maybe it's the sound of your favorite piece of music playing softly.

Allow scents to fill your sacred space, creating an atmosphere of calm.

Is it the fragrance of blooming flowers from your garden, the warm aroma of a candle, or the fresh scent of herbs?

How does being in this space make you feel?

Notice the peace, relaxation, and even the inspiration it brings.

Allow yourself to fully experience the comfort and safety of this personal retreat within your home or yard.

Reflect on the emotions you want to cultivate in this space.

Do you wish to feel calm, safe, comforted, or rejuvenated, perhaps inspired, or simply grounded?

As you continue breathing deeply, let these emotions envelop you.

Remember, this sacred space is always accessible to you.

You can return here in your mind whenever you need a moment of tranquility or reflection.

When you're ready, bring your focus back to your breath.

Take a deep breath in and slowly release it.

Begin to bring awareness to your fingers and toes, gradually returning to your physical surroundings.

When you feel ready, open your eyes, carrying the peace of your sacred space with you as you continue your day.

• • • •

Reflect on your visualized sacred space and consider whether you can re-create it, or a version of it, in your home. If possible, take steps to do so. Creating a personal and private space can promote both external and internal peace, benefiting you and those around you.

Deepening the Self-Care Experience

Once you establish a space where you feel safe and uninterrupted, you'll likely find that other forms of self-care naturally deepen. Breathing exercises, body scans, guided meditation—these practices become more effective when your nervous system isn't constantly expecting the next interruption. It's not just about the act itself; it's about the environment in which you're doing it. When your body feels truly alone, safe, and at ease, you can immerse yourself more fully. The noise quiets down, and the static clears away.

And in that quiet, something beautiful happens: You begin to hear yourself again.

You might notice what you've been pushing aside. You might feel emotions that have been bubbling beneath the surface. You might suddenly experience a creative idea or a sexual fantasy popping up seemingly out of nowhere. That's not coincidence. That's your inner world finally having space to express itself.

This is also where sexual self-care flourishes—not in performance, but in presence. From this deep connection with yourself, everything else begins to shift. Your choices, desires, and confidence—all evolve. You're no longer merely surviving; you're nurturing, selecting, and crafting something that truly belongs to you.

Taking a Break

We live in a culture that praises persistence: push through, try harder, and don't give up. While that kind of grit can be useful in certain areas or times in our life—such as work, training for a marathon, or learning a new skill—it's not always the solution in our personal lives, especially when it comes to sex.

Sometimes in our sex lives, when things aren't working, the impulse is to double down, to keep trying the same approach in hopes that one day it'll magically work. However, more effort doesn't always lead to better outcomes; in fact, sometimes it's the opposite. As Einstein (playfully but pointedly) put it, "Insanity is doing the same thing over and over again and expecting different results." Sometimes, the smartest move isn't to try harder—but to try something different.

What if you took a moment to pause instead of pushing harder?

What if the most loving and intelligent thing you could do for yourself—or your relationship—was to stop? Just for a moment. Just long enough to breathe. To reconnect in ways that have nothing to do with sex. To remember why you enjoy each other. To laugh, share meals, take walks, or binge-watch.

In couples work, I often suggest exactly this: Take a breather. A temporary reset. Not because something is damaged—but because it needs space—to soften and remember that there is more to the relationship than the pressure to perform, fix, or figure it all out.

When sex feels strained, it tends to consume all the oxygen in the room. It becomes the unspeakable topic behind every argument, every cold shoulder, every teary-eyed "I'm fine." Suddenly, a forgotten errand or an offhand comment escalates into a full-blown fight—and beneath it all, the true wound is unmet needs or unspoken fear.

Taking a break doesn't mean you're giving up. It means you're tuning in. You're saying, "Let's stop doing what isn't working and shift our focus for a while." When you relieve the pressure on the sexual part of your connection, it allows the rest of the relationship room to breathe—and often, that alone can work wonders.

You may find moments of affection returning on their own. You may laugh more. You may even miss each other and feel that familiar flutter of anticipation again. From that place, you can check in: *Where are we now? What do we want next?* And that's when change begins to feel like possibility rather than punishment.

The R Word (Rest. Yes, Rest.)

Let's discuss a word that many of us struggle with: *rest*.

Rest is often viewed as a luxury—or worse, a weakness. It's something we do once we've "earned it," something set aside for vacation, retirement, or some distant future when everything on the to-do list is finally checked off.

But true rest isn't merely the absence of activity; it's accompanied by the presence of permission. Permission to stop and be a little unproductive. To refrain from trying to fix anything or anyone and . . . just be.

Rest isn't the same as taking a break. A break is a shift in focus—even stepping away from sex can lead to prioritizing connection in other ways. However, rest serves as its own form of nourishment. It involves quieting the mental noise, releasing the emotional weight, and allowing your body, mind, and nervous system to reset.

Rest is radical. It's a refusal to let exhaustion be your baseline. And it's essential—especially when you're exploring something as nuanced and vulnerable as your sexual well-being.

Rest doesn't mean abandoning your intentions; it means pausing to let them settle in. You can still keep your plan and your desires. You're not throwing anything away—you're simply setting it aside for now so you can return with greater clarity, more softness, and perhaps even a touch of humor. Because perspective is a powerful thing.

You might return to your plan and find that you actually feel hopeful again, or less overwhelmed, or suddenly inspired to try something new. Or—surprise—you might discover that the tension that once felt unmovable has begun to dissolve. That's the thing about rest: It doesn't solve everything, but it changes everything.

Eyes Wide Open

When we take space—whether through breaks, rest, or quiet moments alone—we give ourselves a chance to see with new eyes. Maybe you notice your partner's tenderness again, or you realize that you're not as angry as you thought. Perhaps what you needed all along wasn't some grand solution, but just time. Time to remember yourself and let the noise settle. Time to feel safe again. Often, that new clarity arrives not through effort, but through stillness.

Your nervous system, that brilliant inner compass, understands the difference between forced connection and genuine, grounded intimacy. It softens when it knows you're safe and opens when it's no longer on high alert.

That's why sacred space, rest, and intentional breaks aren't merely luxuries; they're practices—practices of self-trust, self-kindness, and long-term love. They enable us to return to our relationships not with gritted teeth, but with open hearts.

You don't need to have everything figured out. You just need to take care of yourself along the way. You're allowed to pause and rest. You're allowed to take a breath. And when and if you're ready, you can begin again.

Sexual Self-Care
(Yes, of course we're going to talk more about sexual self-care!)

Sexual self-care isn't merely a side dish on the menu of our well-being—it's a delectable part of the main course. When we discuss self-care, we often overlook that our sexual selves are part of the whole package. Just like our emotional health, physical state, and spiritual vitality, our sexuality requires attention, affection, and space to flourish.

Sex is more than just an act. It's an expression of who we are and how we feel in our own skin. It reflects what we believe we deserve, how we communicate, and how we connect with others. It's both the mirror and the message. When we engage in sexual self-care, we're not only nurturing our bodies—we're also tuning in to the joy of our longings, beliefs, and boundaries.

Sexual self-care involves getting to know your own body, all of it—even the parts we were told to ignore or name in whispers. What feels good? What doesn't? What gives you a shiver of delight? What feels uncomfortable? Understanding your own turn-ons and turn-offs is the foundation of sexual self-love. Communication plays a major role in this. Sharing your desires, curiosities, and your "no thank yous" with a partner (or even just with yourself) is one of the most nurturing—and clearest—things you can do. But those boundaries aren't fixed. They can change over time, with experience, or depending on your mood. Talk about them with your partner and revisit them often. That's all part of self-care.

Another important part of self-care is checking on your health. Getting regular reproductive care, doing STI tests, and asking questions about how your body is changing (hello, menopause, hormonal shifts, or new medications) are all vital aspects of sexual self-care. There's no shame in staying informed—it's empowering.

And we're not leaving here until we talk about masturbation. Solo sex is more than just a stress reliever (though it's great for that, too). It offers a powerful, private space to connect with your body, explore pleasure, and remind yourself that you are fully capable of your own pleasure. It encourages blood flow, natural lubrication, better sleep, and boosts our "feel-good" hormones. It's essentially medicine that doesn't require a prescription.

Exploring your interests—whether that's reading erotica or trying out a new toy or lube—can be part of the experience. Not everything will be your cup of tea, and that's okay. The goal is exploration. Pleasure doesn't have to be productive (remember the "rest" section?).

Sometimes, sexual self-care involves asking for help. If you're navigating differences in desire with a partner, dealing with body image issues, gender identity, struggling with compulsive behaviors, or healing from trauma, speaking with a certified sex therapist can be a powerful act of love toward yourself. Seeking support is not a sign of failure—it's a tool for deeper understanding and healing.

And finally, let's get real about the stories we're consuming. If porn is part of your routine, that's okay, but it's important to remember that it's fantasy, not guidance. Just like Hollywood rom-coms don't mirror real-life relationships, adult films aren't visual manuals for healthy, mutually satisfying sex. Maintaining realistic expectations—and being honest about what serves you and what doesn't—is a subtle but powerful form of self-awareness.

Sexual self-care and self-love are not luxuries. They are essential to returning home to ourselves—body, mind, heart, and pleasure included.

Chapter 5

Lady Parts ~ (Also Known as Anatomy We Deserve to Understand)

Let's clarify something right away: The word *vagina* has been doing too much heavy lifting. Usually, when people say "vagina," they're actually referring to the *vulva*—the collection of parts visible on the outside. The vagina itself is just one part of the puzzle, like the hallway inside the front door. The vulva? That's the entire front porch, the welcome mat, and, yes, the party that happens on the lawn.

And here's the beautiful part: No two vulvas look exactly alike. Some are compact, while others are more spacious; some are tucked in, and others are proudly extroverted. Colors range from pale pink to deep chocolate brown. They also change over time—like a face that gains character with each passing year. Every single one is normal.

The Labia

Think of the labia as the "curtains" of the stage. The outer lips (labia majora) are usually fleshier and often have pubic hair after puberty. The inner lips (labia minora) sit just inside and meet at the clitoris. They can be long, short, or even slightly asymmetrical. Sometimes one takes center stage more than the other, and that's perfectly natural. When aroused, the labia fill with blood and become more sensitive, which is their way of saying, "The show is about to start."

The Clitoris

Ah, the headliner. The tip of the clitoris (the glans) sits right where the inner lips meet, often peeking out from beneath its little hood. It may be tiny or more prominent—size doesn't matter here. What matters is that this is the only organ in the human body designed solely for pleasure. Just the tip contains about eight thousand nerve endings—twice as many as a penis.

But don't be fooled by what's visible on the surface. That visible nub is just the tip of an iceberg-sized network of pleasure. Inside, the clitoris branches out in a wishbone shape with roots and legs that embrace the vaginal canal. Overall, it spans about 3.5 to 4.5 inches. If the body were a theme park, the clitoris would be the roller coaster everyone queues up for.

The Openings

Below the clitoris are two small but vital openings. The first is the urethral opening (your body's built-in drainpipe for urine). Just beneath that is the vaginal opening—the gateway for menstrual blood, penetration (toys, fingers, penises), and, yes, babies. Although the vagina receives most of the cultural focus, it's really just one stop on the tour.

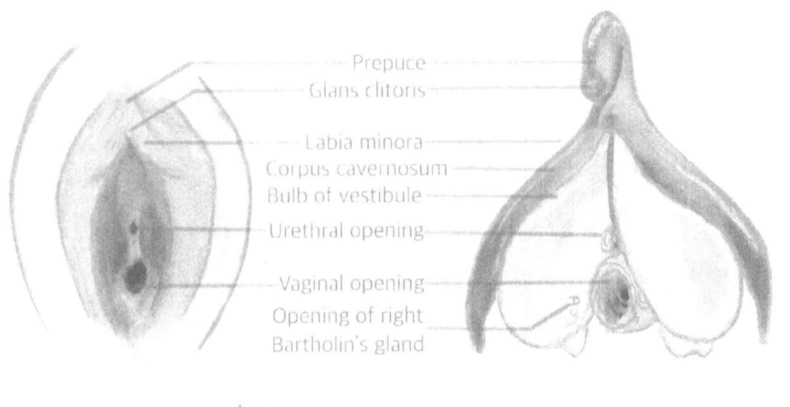

Clitoris interior and exterior

Mons Pubis

Above everything is the mons pubis, the soft mound that cushions the pubic bone. After puberty, it usually grows hair, which—contrary to cultural myths—isn't there to ruin swimsuit season. It's there to provide protection and add another layer of individuality.

The Anus

And finally, let's not forget the neighbor to the south: the anus. With its own set of sensitive nerve endings, it can be a source of pleasure for some people. Like any good neighborly relationship, this one requires respect, communication, and care.

Erogenous Zones

Of course, pleasure doesn't end at the vulva. The body is dotted with erogenous zones like hidden gems on a treasure map, waiting to be discovered. For some, it's the breasts or nipples. For others, it's the neck, ears, or thighs. Context also matters—what makes you melt one night might make you shrug the next.

Genital Hot Spots

Clitoris: This is the undisputed MVP of pleasure, with dense nerve endings and larger-than-life internal structure.

G-Spot: A few inches inside on the front wall of the vagina, sometimes described as feeling slightly spongier or ridged compared to the surrounding tissue. For some, it's a delight; for others, it's a "meh." Both are normal.

Vulva: The labia are highly sensitive. Stroking, pressure, or vibration in this area can be just as pleasurable as direct clitoral stimulation.

Looking at the above descriptions, it's clear that our bodies don't come with a universal "turn-on button." They're more like playlists—highly personal, always changing, and best discovered through exploration and conversation.

Extragenital Erogenous Zones

Pleasure isn't limited to the genitals. Our bodies contain many surprising hot spots—areas that respond wonderfully to touch, attention, and curiosity. These extragenital erogenous zones remind us that intimacy can be a full-body experience.

Head and Neck

The ears are small but powerful. A kiss on the lobe, a warm breath behind the ear, or even a playful whisper can trigger unexpected shivers. The neck is another classic—soft, vulnerable, and endlessly receptive. And lips? They're both messengers and magnets, carrying sensation inward and inviting connection outward.

Mons pubis
Prepuce
Clitoris
Labium majus
Urethral orifice
Labium minus
Vaginal orifice
Perineal raphe
Anus

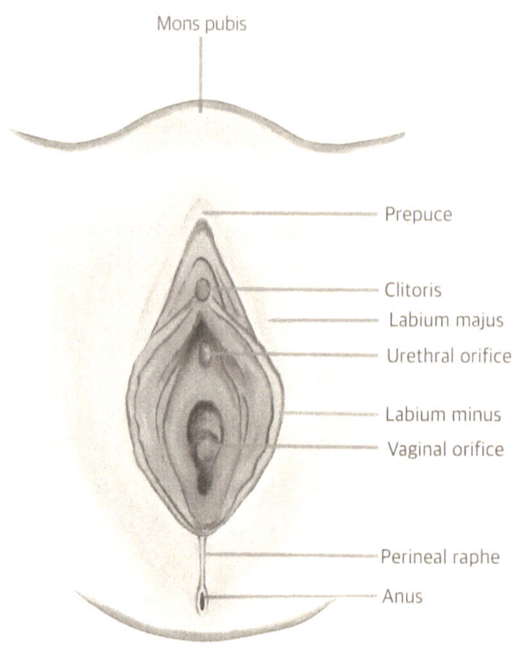

The Vulva

Upper Body

Breasts and nipples are often the first areas that come to mind, but the entire chest can respond to touch. Shoulders, armpits, and even the upper back have the potential for sensation that combines arousal with comfort. Sometimes, what ignites desire isn't the "obvious" spot but those areas that catch us off guard.

Lower Body

The stomach, lower abdomen, and especially the inner thighs can heighten anticipation with even the lightest touch. The buttocks, too, are rich with nerve endings—capable of delivering pleasure that's both grounding and exhilarating.

Limbs

Hands and wrists are surprisingly intimate, often overlooked in the rush toward more obvious areas. Fingers intertwined, palms stroked, or wrists kissed can feel tender and erotic all at once. For some, feet are an absolute no; for others, they're a delicacy—it just depends on the individual palate.

Beyond the Obvious

- **Individuality:** Every body has its own "recipe" for pleasure. What feels electric to one person may not register for another. Both are completely normal.
- **Communication:** The quickest way to learn is by noticing and asking. Breath, movement, and subtle sounds are often the body's way of providing feedback.
- **Experimentation:** There isn't one correct technique. Gentle strokes, firmer pressure, lips, teeth, warmth, coolness—all can be part of the mix. The key is to stay curious, not prescriptive.

The Internal Parts

If the vulva is the dining room—the part set up for guests, easy to see and admire—then the internal organs are the kitchen. Less visible, but equally essential. This is where much of the behind-the-scenes magic occurs: Cycles are regulated, hormones are stirred, sensations are deepened. And just like a kitchen, each part has its own role in the larger recipe of pleasure and reproduction.

The Vagina

The vagina is the entryway from the "front of the house" into the rest of the body. A muscular, stretchable tube, it's designed to be adaptable. When at rest, it's narrow and snug, but when aroused, it expands and lengthens—a response called "tenting." This helps provide comfort during penetration, whether that's fingers, toys, tampons, or penises. It also serves as the passageway for menstrual blood and the route babies take during birth. Despite common myths, nothing can get "lost" in the vagina; it has an endpoint, guarded by the cervix.

The Cervix

The cervix is a small but mighty opening at the end of the vaginal canal, often likened to a tiny donut with a pinhole center. That opening allows menstrual blood to exit the uterus and sperm to enter. During childbirth, the cervix dilates enough for a baby to pass through—a remarkable feat that highlights how impressive this "doorway" can be. For some, touching the cervix feels uncomfortable, while for others, it's part of pleasure. Like any doorway, it holds different meanings depending on who's approaching it.

The Uterus

The uterus—also known as the womb—is the pear-shaped "mixing bowl" of the body—muscular, dynamic, and endlessly adaptable. It is the organ where pregnancy develops, but it does much more than that. During arousal, the lower part of the uterus actually lifts upward (the "tenting" process again), creating more room in the vaginal canal. Throughout a lifetime, the uterus contracts, sheds, expands, and shifts—reminding us that it is not a static organ but a lively, active participant in sexual and reproductive health.

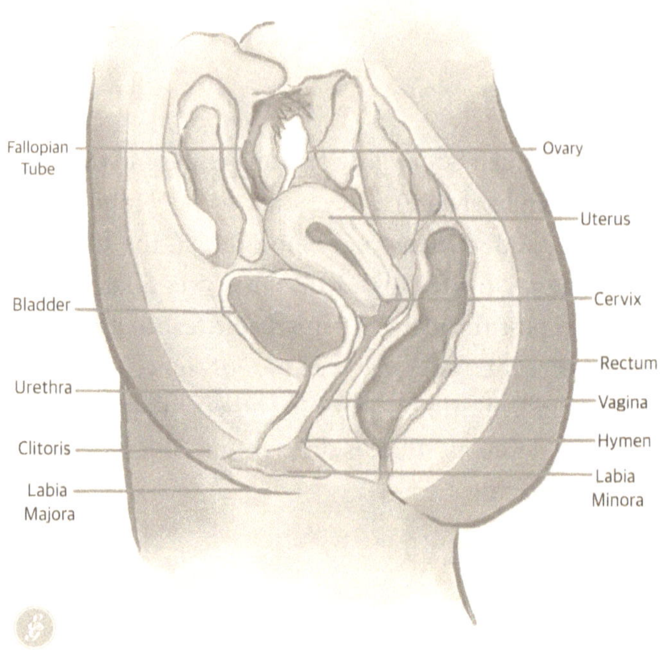

Female Interior

The Fallopian Tubes and Fimbriae

Extending from the uterus like two slender arms, the fallopian tubes serve as pathways for eggs. At their ends are delicate fringes called fimbriae, which wave and guide an egg into the tube when it's released. Sperm travel this route as well, hoping to meet an egg along the way. Think of them as couriers, delivering tiny but essential ingredients for conception.

The Ovaries

On either side of the uterus sit the ovaries—two compact centers of creation and chemistry. They not only store eggs but also produce hormones like estrogen, progesterone, and testosterone. These hormones influence everything from menstrual cycles to moods to libido. Each month (until menopause), the ovaries release an egg—sometimes more than one. They may be small, but their influence is enormous, orchestrating much of the body's rhythm.

Bartholin's Glands

The Bartholin's glands sit just inside the vaginal opening and activate during arousal, providing natural lubrication when you're turned on. They're essentially the body's secret ingredient—a subtle addition that enhances everything for a more satisfying experience.

Skene's Glands

On either side of the urethral opening are the Skene's glands, sometimes called the "female prostate." These glands release fluid that can be part of female ejaculation. They are quiet workers, but ones that can add a surprising flourish to the recipe of arousal.

The Hymen

The hymen is a thin, flexible membrane that partially covers the vaginal opening. Its appearance varies greatly, and contrary to outdated myths, it is *not* a reliable indicator of virginity. Hymens can stretch or tear through physical activity, tampon use, or simple movement. For some, the first experience of vaginal penetration may cause minor tearing or bleeding; for others, it does not. Like every individual, it varies from person to person.

The G-Spot

A few inches inside the vagina, on the front wall, is the G-spot. Some describe it as slightly textured compared to surrounding tissue. For some, stimulation here is intensely pleasurable; for others, it isn't. Both experiences are valid. Think of it less like a "magic button" and more of a unique character—loved by some, unremarkable to others.

Caring for Your External "Lady Parts"

- To soothe vaginal dryness
- To support vaginal health without hormones
- To choose the right moisturizing lubricants

Dryness or vaginal atrophy (thinning of the tissues) can affect comfort, pleasure, and everyday ease. With the right care, you can encourage blood flow, improve flexibility, and support healthier vaginal tissue over time.

Choosing Personal Lubricants

Lubricants aren't just for sex—they can also help restore comfort day to day. I often suggest to my clients to use lubricant daily for soothing and hydrating the vulva. Think of it as a love letter to your "lady parts." Just as you would apply a fabulous serum on your face and neck to support the condition of your skin, this works in a similar way—the more you use it, the better the effect. Place some lubricant on the tips of your fingers (just a little amount can go a long way) and gently smooth or pat it into your vulva tissue. You can also add a small amount at the opening of the vagina.

A good product should only contain high-quality ingredients and will either:

Add moisture (bring hydration into the skin and tissue), or
Seal in moisture (hold that hydration in place so it lasts longer)

There are three types of lubricants—water-based lubricants, which are versatile, easy to clean, and safe with latex condoms and most sex toys; silicone-based lubricants, which are longer-lasting than water-based lubricants and hypoallergenic for most, water-resistant, and safe with latex condoms; and oil-based lubricants, which are also long-lasting, helpful in improving the condition of your skin, but will damage latex condoms and silicone-material sex toys. And then there are moisturizers—not the same as lubricants, but great for the lady parts, too.

Let's talk about natural oils. There are many that can be helpful, such as pure or virgin coconut oil, known for moisturizing tissue and potentially containing antibacterial and antifungal properties. Almond oil, olive oil, and sunflower seed oil are all rich in vitamin E and can help nourish the skin. Although I am a big fan of natural and clean products, I will say that using natural oils alone sometimes doesn't provide the same effect as a high-quality lubricant that contains some of these natural oils but also other premium ingredients, which can create a recipe for the best of both worlds.

Sweet spot tip: Moisturizers and sealants work best together. Moisturizers soak the skin like a refreshing drink, while sealants lock in that moisture. Together, they keep vaginal tissue more supple, resilient, and prepared for comfort—in everyday life *and* in pleasure.

I can't emphasize enough how important it is to use only high-quality, clean products. Review the ingredients in your products—you deserve the very best, and your body will thank you for it.

A good lubricant should never feel sticky or "goopy." It should glide smoothly and maintain a consistent texture throughout use. You might prefer a thinner lubricant that mimics your body's natural lubrication, or a thicker formula that provides extra cushioning and reduces friction during stimulation. There's no right or wrong choice—it's all about what feels best for you. But no matter your preference, quality is nonnegotiable.

Unfortunately, many products on the market are packed with ingredients that do more harm than good. That's why I recommend choosing a formula that's rich, nourishing, and made from nature's most potent ingredients—designed to hydrate, soothe, and protect your most sensitive skin.

Look for lubricants infused with oils like aloe vera, jojoba, coconut, and sea buckthorn, paired with water-based minerals such as magnesium. These ingredients can revitalize and strengthen vulvar tissue, support collagen production, and enhance elasticity. Hyaluronic acid is also a powerful ally, helping the skin retain moisture and stay supple.

When shopping for vaginal moisturizers, keep an eye out for ingredients that promote collagen and elastin production —like sodium hyaluronate—and nourishing oils and vitamins including sea buckthorn oil, aloe, jojoba, coconut oil, vitamin E, and magnesium.

Just as important is what you *don't* want: Steer clear of lubricants that contain glycerin, parabens, petroleum or mineral oils, synthetic hormones, alcohols, and added fragrance. These can disrupt your natural balance, trap bacteria, damage condoms and toys, and cause irritation or infection. Even flavored, warming, or cooling lubricants—though much improved in recent years—can still be irritating for some users.

Beyond physical comfort, using lubricant can enhance a positive, pleasurable experience. When sex feels good—comfortable, smooth, and free of pain—you're more likely to look forward to it, and that anticipation alone can heighten arousal and natural lubrication. The mind–body connection is powerful, and a simple product like lubricant can be an easy yet meaningful tool in creating a more enjoyable and satisfying sexual experience.

Mind–body connection: Using lubricant can indirectly support your potential for heightened arousal and lubrication response. This can then lead to positively anticipating sex, as an enjoyable activity rather than one of discomfort.

Self-Pleasuring for Women

Let's talk about self-pleasure. Yes, that thing most of us learned early on was "bad," "dirty," or "something you just don't do," and something to feel shameful and guilty about. The word *masturbation* was first used in the 1600s, surrounded by religious and cultural disapproval. But the truth is, branding something as sinful doesn't magically make it harmful.

Your body was created with built-in pleasure systems. Touching your skin, increasing blood flow, activating nerve endings—these are normal, healthy functions. We appreciate them when we massage lotion into our hands or rub our shoulders after a long day. No one looks at you massaging your palm and says, "Careful, that's morally corrupt." Sexual self-touch is no different.

There's no single "correct" way to pleasure yourself. If it feels good, doesn't hurt, and doesn't make you late for work—then enjoy. Self-pleasure is simply a way to know your body better, deepen your comfort with desire, and nurture the most enduring relationship you'll ever have: the one you have with yourself.

In a book called *Nothing Is Off the Table*, we'd be remiss not to mention this: Your own body belongs squarely on the menu.

Why?

Yes, it feels good—but it also:

> Strengthens and exercises pelvic floor muscles
> Revitalizes tissues by boosting blood flow
> Enhances immune function (thanks to hormone shifts after orgasm)
> Eases insomnia
> Lifts mood and reduces depression
> Lessens menstrual discomfort
> Releases stress and tension

Self-pleasure is also a private classroom. It helps you learn what turns you on, without worrying about anyone else's expectations. You can experiment with arousal, discover pathways to orgasm, or simply enjoy sensation for its own sake. And what you learn alone becomes a gift you can share with a partner, whether that's guiding their touch or expanding your sexual repertoire together.

It's also practical. If your partner is tired, unwell, or simply not in sync with your rhythm, you can still meet your own needs. Self-pleasure isn't a substitute for intimacy with someone else; it's part of your intimacy with yourself. It's normal and very healthy—and one of the most affirming ways to remind yourself that your body is worthy of attention, curiosity, and joy.

Libido

Libido is one of those words that gets thrown around quite a bit, often in whispers, jokes, or moments of panic: *Do I have enough? Do I have too little? Where did it go?* But at its core, libido simply means sexual desire—the mental nudge that prompts you toward wanting sex initially. It's the mind's way of saying, "*Hey, let's play.*"

Technically, psychologists define libido as a kind of psychic (mental) energy—impulses that originate from the mind. But most of us understand it as that tingling sensation of desire, the thought or image that stirs something inside us, or the warm rush that makes us curious for more. Sometimes it starts in the body—a pulse in your groin that causes you to lean in. Other times, it begins in the mind—a memory, a fantasy, a scent, or a touch from a partner that makes your whole being light up.

Why Does It Come and Go?

Libido isn't a machine; it's more like a considerate houseguest: It arrives when conditions feel right and often leaves when you're tired, stressed, distracted, or unwell. Your brain is wired to prioritize survival first, pleasure second. So, if you're juggling deadlines, dinner, or daycare, your mind might say, "*Sex? Not tonight. We've got other things to deal with.*"

This mismatch becomes especially evident when one partner's brain is thinking, *I feel sexy—let's go*, while the other is making a to-do list.

Sound familiar?

The Arc of Desire

Libido is usually high at the start of a relationship—that intoxicating glue that pulls you together. Over time (usually six months to two years), it tends to settle into a steadier rhythm. This change often makes people nervous, but it's completely normal. Honestly, if you kept up the same pace as those first few months, when would you eat, sleep, or pay the bills?

Libido also responds to changes in the body. Hormones, illness, pregnancy, menopause, birth control, and certain medications (especially antidepressants) can all affect it. If you suspect this is the case, a healthcare provider can help you understand what's happening. Even when a medical factor is involved, desire can often be nurtured through care, patience, and curiosity.

Libido is also influenced by the quality of your relationship with yourself and your partner. If there is a lack of self-care and rest, unresolved hurt feelings and resentments, or insufficient quality time and effort, or an imbalance of responsibilities, your libido is likely to be affected.

Libido does not exist in isolation; it is influenced by our internal thoughts, emotions, well-being, and personal circumstances like relationships, stress, and energy levels.

Why Do My Partner and I Have Different Levels of Libido?

Because you're different people. Some of us are wired to think about sex often; others rarely do unless something sparks the idea. Stress, health, recent sexual experiences, cultural messages, and even genetics all play a role. Differences in libido are among the most common dynamics in relationships. Sometimes they're temporary—a blip during illness or stress. And sometimes they're ongoing.

The key isn't to "fix" your partner's libido (spoiler—you can't). It's to discover together how to meet both of your needs with respect and creativity.

What's Normal?

There is no such thing as a "normal" libido. It is individual, changing, and always shifting. It only becomes an issue if it causes you distress or interferes with the sex life you want. If you (and your partner, if you have one) are comfortable with your level of desire, then you have nothing to worry about—period.

The Feedback Loop of Pleasure

One thing researchers and therapists agree on: The more positive sexual experiences you have—solo or with a partner—the more likely your libido is to show up. Pleasure builds on itself. When sex feels safe, comfortable, and satisfying, desire and positive anticipation tend to emerge more often. This means that sometimes, paradoxically, the best way to find libido is to give it a chance to develop rather than waiting for it to lead. And here's something to look forward to: The more you have sex, the more you want it.

Orgasms for Women

If desire is the appetizer, sexual pleasure is the main course, followed by the grand dessert, the orgasm. This is what people often envision when they think of sex. But here's the point: Orgasms are not guaranteed—they are diverse, unpredictable, and often surprising. Some are intense, some are subtle, and some don't happen at all. They are not a measure of sexual success, nor are they the only way to experience pleasure.

Anatomy of an Orgasm

When it comes to female pleasure, the clitoris is the head chef. As described above, beyond its tip is actually a structure about four inches in total length, curving back like a wishbone. With thousands of nerve endings and its sole purpose being pleasure, it's the master behind most orgasms.

What Happens in the Body

Orgasms are fundamentally a reflex. With enough arousal and stimulation, the brain interprets sensation as pleasurable and signals the body to increase blood flow, swell tissues, and boost sensitivity. As stimulation continues, the pelvic floor muscles begin to contract rhythmically—a series of involuntary pulses that usually last ten to fifteen seconds.

The experience can feel like anything from fireworks to a gentle wave. Some orgasms feel intense and consuming; others are more delicate, a flicker of release before calm settles in. What follows is often a sense of deep relaxation and contentment—what many describe as the "afterglow."

The Mind Game

Here's where things become complex. Orgasm doesn't occur by willpower; it happens when body and mind collaborate. Stress, distraction, body image worries, or pressure to "perform" can all hijack the process. Relaxation and curiosity help keep the stage clear for arousal to develop.

The plateau phase—that point of being *almost there*—is often misunderstood. Many women think they're stuck or failing. In reality, the plateau can be incredibly enjoyable on its own, like simmering a sauce until it's ready to bubble over.

Self-Pleasure as a Guide

Exploring your body on your own is one of the most effective ways to learn what kind of touch, pace, and intensity feel best for you. Self-pleasure offers the freedom to experiment without pressure, performance anxiety, or outside expectations. And what you discover during solo exploration can be a gift to share with a partner—not as a strict script they must follow, but as a map of what tends to bring you the most pleasure.

Orgasms can change over time, often becoming easier at some points in life and more elusive at others.

Factors like hormones, age, stress, illness, medications, or relationship changes can all affect this. None of these shifts suggest a problem—they simply reflect how your body adapts. Sometimes, the route to orgasm evolves and calls for new approaches.

Expanding Pleasure

If you want to enhance your orgasmic experience, trying different things can be helpful. As mentioned earlier, exploring various erogenous zones, experimenting with vibrators or new types of touch, or gradually building arousal before focusing on the genitals can all make the experience more intense. Some find that delaying orgasm—pushing themselves to the edge, then calming down—can increase the strength of the final release. For others, having frequent orgasms helps maintain desire and keeps sensitivity high.

And this bears repeating (because it's important!): Orgasm isn't the only goal. Many women find that the period of arousal, connection, and sensation leading up to orgasm is the most rewarding part of sex. Focusing less on the "finish line" often makes orgasm more likely—and even when it doesn't arrive, pleasure itself is still meaningful.

Learning Through Exploration

If you want to enhance your orgasms, strengthening your pelvic floor muscles can help (see below). Kegel exercises—contracting and relaxing the same muscles you use to stop urine midstream—can make contractions during orgasm feel more intense. (Sidenote: Don't hold your urine midstream unless a medical professional has advised you to do so.) Equally important as tightening is learning to relax these muscles, which helps keep them flexible and responsive.

Experimentation is another ally. Try giving more time for arousal to build, whether alone or with a partner. Sometimes, arousal occurs more easily when the whole body is invited into the experience.

What Is the Pelvic Floor?

Think of your pelvic floor as a kind of hammock or sling made of muscle, sitting at the base of your pelvis. It's not just one muscle but a team—about fourteen muscles layered together, working in harmony to support and facilitate movement. This "hammock" supports the organs in your pelvis—your bladder, uterus, intestines—while still leaving space for important openings like the urethra, vagina, and anus.

A healthy pelvic floor is both strong *and* flexible. These muscles can contract when needed, relax at will, and respond smoothly to daily rhythms. Like other muscles in the body, pelvic floors vary in appearance and sensation from person to person.

So, what does this set of muscles actually do? Quite a bit.

> They are the origin of the pulsating, enjoyable contractions during orgasm—and yes, stronger muscles often enhance the intensity of orgasms.
> They help the body relax enough for comfortable vaginal penetration, whether that's with a partner, a toy, or even during a medical exam.

They keep urine inside your bladder when you laugh, cough, sneeze, or jump.

They hold stool in the rectum until you decide it's time to go.

In short, your pelvic floor is partly a pleasure-maker, partly a gatekeeper, and partly a stabilizer.

When Things Go Off-Balance

Some people move through life without giving their pelvic floor a second thought. Others notice issues—like leaking when they cough or sneeze, pain during penetration, difficulty reaching orgasm, or a feeling of heaviness or pressure. These problems often stem from the muscles being too weak, too tight, not flexible enough, or not functioning properly. Sometimes it's a combination of all of these factors.

The good news is your pelvic floor can be trained. With awareness, exercises, and support from practices like physical therapy, mindful relaxation, or intentional strengthening, you can prevent issues or improve existing ones. Like any other part of your body, these muscles respond beautifully when you give them proper care and attention.

(See the website for further pelvic floor information—and Kegel exercises)

Your "Homework"

Think of orgasm exploration as research—not a test. The invitation is to discover what your body enjoys rather than reaching a predetermined outcome. You might try holding off or delaying an orgasm to see how sensation builds, or you might practice giving yourself permission to orgasm at your own pace, without pressure. Share what you learn with a partner by inviting them on a "sensual tour" of your body—and then trade places.

Above all, keep in mind that orgasm is just one aspect of a much broader "menu" of pleasure.

Chapter 6

The Pleasure Is Yours

You are responsible for your own pleasure. That might seem like a lot of pressure, depending on your perspective. But here's the truth: No one else can do this for you. Your partner can meet you there, certainly. But they can't read your mind, interpret your needs, or ignite your desire without your participation. That's *your* job—and that's a good thing.

Let's start by exploring the realities that can diminish our desire. Libido doesn't exist in a vacuum—it's deeply connected to how we feel in our bodies, minds, and lives. If your body is experiencing chronic pain, hormonal shifts, fatigue, or medication side effects, your desire may be muted. If your mind is overwhelmed with a never-ending to-do list, managing stress, or running scripts of shame or guilt around sex, your erotic energy doesn't simply vanish—it becomes suppressed.

Lifestyle factors like nutrition, movement, sleep, and substance use also matter. These aren't moral judgments—they're part of the ecology of your sexual self; everything is connected. Just as we don't expect ourselves to sprint up a mountain without eating, sleeping, or stretching, we can't expect to feel sensual, alive, and responsive without caring for the context.

So, yes, you are in charge. But not in the "you should be doing more" kind of way, but rather in the "you get to reclaim this" kind of way.

The Power of Asking

One of the most powerful acts of sexual self-care is naming what you want. And I'm not talking about hinting or hoping. It might mean saying, "I'd love more foreplay," or "I need more time to get turned on," or "I'm curious about trying this." It might also mean saying, "I don't like that," or "Let's do this instead."

Often, women are conditioned to prioritize others' pleasure before their own. We're told not to be "too much." We're afraid to seem needy, demanding, or—heaven forbid—nagging. (That word consistently upsets me—especially when it's used to dismiss women.) But here's the truth: Expressing your needs isn't nagging. It's clarity. It's trust. It's honoring your own body enough to speak up for it.

And if your desires feel unclear to you, that's okay. Owning your pleasure also means taking the time to discover it. You are not a vending machine. You don't press a button and instantly get what you want. You are a living, breathing, evolving being—and your pleasure will evolve, too.

Worthiness and Permission

There's often a quiet narrative running beneath the surface: "Do I deserve this?" Or, "Is it acceptable to want this?" Whether it's an orgasm, a long kiss, a night off, or even the simple freedom to want something—many of us hesitate and wait for permission. Often, it's because we hope someone else will offer it. But your worthiness is not up for debate. You don't earn pleasure like a reward; you claim it because you are human, and humans are wired for joy.

Give yourself permission. Not just for sex, but for play, curiosity, rest, and certainly for wanting more.

What Are *You* Getting Out of It?

Let's talk about investment. If you're consistently engaging in sexual experiences that don't offer you much in return—whether it's pleasure, connection, closeness, or validation—it's natural that your desire would wane. Desire needs a reason to return. We can only go to the well so many times if it keeps coming up dry.

That's why it's worth checking in: *What do I get from this experience? What am I giving? What do I need more (or less) of? What would make this feel more reciprocal?*

Pleasure isn't just about what you do—it's about how it feels. It's not solely about orgasm. It's about how your partner looks at you, listens, and helps you fulfil your needs. It's also about the way your skin tingles under their touch and the sense of being lovingly embraced. When those elements are missing, the "dish" may fall flat. None of that is your fault—it's simply information.

One of the most transformative sessions I've experienced focused on a simple yet radical truth: Pleasure is each person's own responsibility. For many, that idea initially feels heavy, but in reality, it is profoundly freeing—it unlocks both self-awareness and connection. Maria and James came to me feeling distant from each other, unsure how to rekindle intimacy. I introduced the idea that each person is responsible for their own pleasure—not in isolation, but as an act of self-awareness that enriches the relationship.

For Maria, this was new. She'd spent years believing that fulfillment meant her partner should instinctively "know" what she needed. But no one is a mind reader. We discussed that communicating desire is an act of self-advocacy, not selfishness. The first step is reflecting on what creates desire and enjoyment for ourselves. This awareness allows us to articulate what we need to our partner. In the case of Maria and James, Maria felt exhausted and stretched thin by life's demands. She looked to James to identify and provide the elements to create desire for her, instead of looking within herself. James, meanwhile, wanted to be supportive and create pleasurable experiences for Maria, but didn't know how. Together, we explored how stress and unspoken needs can quietly dim desire. I encouraged them to start small—every week, they would each share a want that they felt would create pleasure and desire for them, no matter how simple.

When they returned, Maria admitted that waiting for the "right mood" had been a lifelong habit. Now, she was learning that readiness wasn't about waiting—it was about creating. I invited them to think of intimacy like setting a table: You can choose the lighting, the music, and the atmosphere that invites connection. They started taking turns planning intentional, pressure-free evenings—spaces for curiosity rather than performance. They realized that pleasure isn't a goal to chase—it's a living, evolving conversation between two people learning to listen . . . and trust. Their relationship began to transform.

Rather than focusing on grand gestures, it was about simple, honest conversations that brought them closer than ever before.

How to Ask for What You Need (Without Feeling like a Burden, a Buzzkill, or a Broken Record)

It's easy to fall into the trap of thinking your partner should automatically know what you want. Spoiler: They don't. Even the most attentive, loving partners aren't mind readers. And even if they were last week, people (and preferences) change.

Here's a simple way to start the conversation:

- **Begin with the positive. Try saying:** "I really love when you . . ." or "Last time, what felt amazing to me was . . ."
- **Be specific. Swap vague for vivid:** "I'd love more kissing before we move to anything else," or "Slower touch helps me stay in my body."
- **Use curiosity. Invite exploration:** "I've been thinking about trying . . ." or "What would you think about . . . ?"
- **Let go of performance or perfectionism.** You don't have to communicate your desires perfectly. You're learning from each other in real time, and that's part of the enjoyment.
- **Remember: It's a request, not a demand.** You're opening a door, not delivering an ultimatum. It's all in the delivery.

You are allowed to have preferences. You are allowed to ask. And you are allowed to tweak things until they work for both of you.

Are You Ready Yet?

We often wait for the stars to align before allowing ourselves to feel "ready" for sex. The kitchen must be spotless. The kids need to be asleep—and ideally enrolled in college. Our bodies should feel exactly right, our to-do list completely conquered, and our minds utterly clear. The lighting must be just right. The mood is magazine-quality perfect . . . and our partner? They are reading our mind, of course.

But what if readiness wasn't a fixed point on a checklist? What if it didn't require perfection? What if, instead, readiness was something you could *nurture*?

The truth is, many of us have been taught that sexual desire should strike like a lightning bolt—sudden, intense, unmistakable. But for many of us (especially when we're managing households, jobs, responsibilities, hormones, and inner monologues), desire doesn't knock down the door. It waits patiently on the porch . . . maybe with a cake—or a charcuterie board— hoping you'll invite it in.

Sometimes, readiness isn't a *feeling* that shows up. It's a *practice* we ease into.

It might begin with a shift in your breathing, the kind that reconnects you with your body. Or five quiet minutes alone in your room—no obligations, no one needing anything, just you and your own rhythm. Readiness could look like dimming the lights and playing your favorite song. It might mean applying body oil that smells like vacation and makes you feel a little more like yourself. It could also be shifting the internal script from "I should be doing this" to "I get to enjoy this."

That little semantic shift? It's everything.

"I get to."

Yes, you've heard it in a previous chapter . . . but it bears repeating, as those three little words soften the edges and open the door, turning pressure into possibility.

Readiness doesn't mean you're already turned on. It simply means you're willing to show up, notice, and see what unfolds. Maybe you're not hungry for the entire meal, but could you enjoy an appetizer? Could you just be curious about what's on the menu?

It's okay if you don't feel spontaneous or fiery. And it's okay if your body takes a while to catch up to your mind—or the other way around. You can start slowly and stop if you want. You're allowed to say, "*Not yet,*" or "*Maybe later,*" or "*Let's just see where this goes.*"

And most importantly, you can create conditions where pleasure can emerge. Because readiness isn't something you wait for; it's something you *cultivate.*

Set the mood, but also set your intention. Not to perform or deliver, but to *feel.* To notice what your body wants and remember that your pleasure doesn't have to look the same every time.

The stars don't have to align. You don't need to fit a preconceived idea of what pleasure is. You only need to arrive. And perhaps, in that small act of arriving without expectation, readiness finally finds you.

Create a Sexual Recipe

I often tell my clients that creating great sex is like making a recipe. You gather the ingredients, review the recipe (perhaps with a partner), and take a moment to slow down and set the scene—just as you would before preparing a beautiful meal. You don't rush into the kitchen and toss things together blindly. You pause. You plan. You ask yourself: *What am I craving? What do I need to get ready? What ingredients do I already have?*

Sexual pleasure works the same way.

There's no single right way to enjoy sex—just as there's no perfect recipe for everyone, every time. Some nights, you might seek the comfort of something familiar. Other times, you might want to experiment, try something bold, or go all out with a multi-course experience. What matters is that it feels right for *you*, in this moment, with your energy, your body, and your desires, exactly as they are.

The following recipe card isn't about performance; it's about tuning in and giving yourself permission to be curious and playful. It encourages you to take stock of what feels good, what you want to try, and what you might want to leave off the menu for now. It's also a reminder that you can *adjust* the recipe by turning down the heat or adding more spice. You get to choose the setting, pacing, and rhythm that work for *you*.

Think of this as an invitation to gather your ingredients and experiment. Savor the flavors of your own version of pleasure—whether it's slow and sensual, quick and playful, or deeply connected.

The pleasure is yours to create. So go ahead and make it delicious.

Your Sexual Recipe

Yields: One beautifully embodied experience
Prep Time: As long as it takes
Cook Time: Variable—follow your appetite
Pairs Well With: Curiosity, candlelight, and possibly dark chocolate

Ingredients

> 1 comfortable, interruption-free space
> A pinch of privacy, a full scoop of permission
> Several long, deliberate breaths
> 2 tablespoons of trust in your body
> Optional: a playlist, your favorite oil or toy
> A whisper of anticipation
> A warm memory, or a fresh fantasy
> A shake of silliness, a drizzle of boldness
> A handful of sensory focus (touch, smell, sound, taste, sight)
> A slow-simmered "yes."

Instructions

1. **Preheat your presence.** Turn off notifications. Lock the door.
2. **Layer your ingredients.** Add lighting that you love, clothing that makes you feel sexy (or none at all), and a mindset that says, *This time is mine.*
3. **Stir in intention.** Ask: "What do I want to feel right now?" "What is my body whispering for?"
4. **Taste and adjust.** Slowly . . . Let sensation build—deepening with heat, time, and flavor.

5. **Let things bubble.** Whether it's pleasure, laughter, tears, or stillness—let it rise.
6. **Remove from heat with care.** Allow to simmer down gently.

Optional garnish: A few loving words spoken to yourself aloud; a satisfied sigh; a post-pleasure snack.

Chef's Note: This recipe has no "right" outcome. Sometimes it yields fireworks. Sometimes it tastes like coming home.

$$\bullet \quad \bullet \quad \bullet \quad \bullet$$

Another idea in playing with the concept of recipes is a "Chef's Table." Let's imagine your intimate life as a beautifully curated dining experience. Not in the sense of perfection or formality—but in the sense of intention and creativity. Chef's Table isn't about gourmet ingredients or showy performances. It's about designing an experience that feels deliciously *you* . . . and maybe letting your partner in on the magic.

At an authentic Chef's Table, the chef plans the meal, chooses the ingredients, and invites you into their process. You get to taste something thoughtful, surprising, and customized for the moment. What if your intimate life had moments like that—where one of you takes the lead and says, "Tonight, I've got this," and then crafts something playful, sensual, or innovative based on what feels right?

The goal has nothing to do with pressure—it's all about care. The good news is you don't need a culinary degree; you just need some awareness of what you and your partner enjoy, and a willingness to create from that place.

The Chef's Table is about choosing to delight—whether through sensation, surprise, or slow-burning connection. There's no right recipe. Just the invitation to serve—and be served—with intention.

Chef's Table: Your Turn to Curate the Experience

Think of this as an invitation to play with power, presence, and planning. At the Chef's Table, one person takes the lead—not in a domineering way, but in the spirit of generosity and exploration.

Tonight, you're the chef.

(Apron—or clothing—optional.)

Or maybe you're the guest.

(Nothing to do but enjoy . . .)

When you're the chef, you get to design the menu. You choose the vibe, set the pace, and curate the experience with your partner in mind—yes, including their preferences, limits, and desires, but also offering your own flavor of creativity. You might bring in music, lighting, scents, textures, or surprises. You might start with something familiar or introduce something new. (Think: Your signature dish—with a sexy twist.)

When you're the guest, your job is simply to receive. To savor, or offer feedback if needed—but mostly, to relax into the unfolding experience without attempting to steer the ship. Taking turns at the Chef's Table builds trust, imagination, and a sense of shared investment. It's not about doing it "right"—it's about caring enough to plan, to tune in, and to say: "I made this for you."

You don't have to wait for a special occasion. All it takes is intention—and a willingness to show up with an open heart and a taste for connection.

(Warning: It could get messy, or it might be magical—or involve whipped cream. Please don't say I didn't warn you.)

Chapter 7

Mental Foreplay

Where the mind goes, the body follows.

Before our bodies even move, our minds are already in motion. Desire doesn't always start with a kiss or a touch—it can originate from a thought, a smell, a memory, or a whisper of possibility. Mental foreplay is the space between intention and sensation. It's the inner world that builds anticipation, stirs longing, and lays the groundwork for embodied pleasure.

We often think of sex as something that "just happens," but the truth is, we're always rehearsing it in some way—consciously or not. Every time we anticipate a touch, imagine a kiss, or allow ourselves to daydream about pleasure, we're laying neural groundwork. This is where mental foreplay becomes not just playful or sexy, but profoundly healing and expansive.

Therapists and sex researchers understand that imagination is one of our most underutilized tools for sexual well-being.

Psychotherapist Chelsea Wakefield has examined how guided imagery and archetypal work can broaden women's sexual identity, using the concept of an internal "cast of characters" to help clients move beyond restrictive sexual scripts and patterns. I find this quote particularly meaningful: "Many problems in life can be reduced to a failure of imagination. We get stuck in scripts and stories that are too small for the vastness of our souls. . . . The sexual psyche and the range of sexual archetypes available to women are a realm of great potential, largely unexplored."

Mental foreplay invites us to widen those scripts. It encourages curiosity. Instead of defaulting to old stories ("I'm too tired," "I never initiate," "This always goes the same way"), we can imagine new possibilities. Guided imagery, fantasy, and even sensory cues can create an inner shift—one that brings the body along for the ride.

Fantasy doesn't have to be elaborate or theatrical. It can be an image, a sensation, or even a mood—being admired, feeling powerful, completely at ease, or utterly taken care of. It might be an image from a photograph or painting, or the memory of a gaze that made you feel beautiful. This kind of mental engagement doesn't just help prepare us for pleasure—it *is* pleasure.

Guided imagery has long been used in clinical settings to reduce stress, ease anxiety, and improve focus. When combined with intentional sensual awareness, it becomes a powerful gateway to arousal. In fact, studies show that visualization practices enhance blood flow, increase relaxation, and improve sexual desire. Athletes use mental rehearsal to improve performance. Why shouldn't we?

A therapeutic tool I use in my practice is EMDR (Eye Movement Desensitization and Reprocessing)—originally developed for trauma recovery, but also used for a variety of issues, from chronic pain to enhancing sexual health and pleasure. EMDR helps people shift their internal associations, reduce shame, and build future scenarios (called *Future Template work*) that include confidence, calm, and sexual agency. It's not about pretending to be someone you're not. It's about imagining a version of yourself that's more freeing.

What Is EMDR, and Why Does It Matter in Sex Therapy?

Eye Movement Desensitization and Reprocessing—thankfully shortened to EMDR—might sound like something out of a science fiction novel, but its roots are both deeply researched and surprisingly intuitive. At its core, EMDR is a therapeutic approach that helps people heal from trauma—not just major, capital-T events, but also smaller, chronic experiences that linger in the body and shape how we show up in the world, especially in intimate relationships.

EMDR was developed in the late 1980s by Francine Shapiro, a psychologist who noticed—while walking through a park—that her distressing thoughts seemed to soften when her eyes moved back and forth. Intrigued, she began studying the phenomenon and eventually created a protocol that combined eye movements with structured recall of troubling memories. Her early research showed promising results, particularly for people suffering from post-traumatic stress disorder (PTSD). Since then, EMDR has been widely studied, endorsed by organizations like the World Health Organization and the American Psychological Association, and has become a mainstream, evidence-based treatment for trauma.

But what does all of this have to do with sex?

Quite a bit, actually.

Trauma—whether it's sexual, emotional, relational, or medical—often gets stored in the body, quietly shaping our sense of safety, worth, and responsiveness. EMDR helps process those stored memories in a way that allows the nervous system to recalibrate. In other words, it allows the body to finally understand: *That was then. This is now. I'm safe.*

In sex therapy, EMDR can help clients address experiences that affect sexual pleasure and connection. This may include a past assault, ongoing feelings of shame, body image concerns, or early messages about sex that still feel limiting or painful. It can also serve as a tool for exploring more subtle disruptions—moments when someone felt rejected, embarrassed, or unsafe in a sexual context. These memories might not appear as "trauma" in the traditional sense, but they can still influence our libido, arousal, and ability to trust.

The Future Template work that many therapists use focuses not just on healing the past but also on building positive anticipation for the future. In the context of sexual health, that might mean visualizing a desired experience—feeling safe, aroused, playful, or expressive—and using EMDR to anchor that vision in the body and mind. Athletes do this all the time: mentally rehearsing the positive outcome of a game or a routine until their bodies perform effortlessly.

Why not apply the same logic to intimacy?

By helping people reprocess past wounds and adopt new, empowering scripts, EMDR evolves from being merely a trauma treatment to a way of reclaiming sexual agency, attunement, and joy.

Healing isn't just about surviving the past; it's also about creating new stories for the body to believe in.

And let's not forget the sensual power of the senses themselves. Scent—closely linked to memory and emotion—can act as a trigger for relaxation and arousal. The familiar smell of your partner's skin. A perfume that makes you feel like your most sensual self. Even color plays a role. The psychology of color (or chromatics) shows that warm tones can encourage intimacy, while cool tones soothe the nervous system. What you see, smell, and feel in your environment can become part of your sexual script, too.

So mental foreplay isn't about being lost in your head—it's about *coming home* to your body through your imagination. It's about honing the art of anticipation, tuning into your desires, and remembering that the mind is not separate from pleasure—it's a vital part of it.

• • • •

They say the body keeps the score—(and there is a brilliant book by that name by Bessel van der Kolk; I highly recommend it) but the senses write the opening scene.

Before a single word is spoken, before the first brush of skin or flicker of thought, the body begins to tell its story. It starts with a scent, a glance, a shift in temperature, the texture of cotton against the skin or the way light filters through a half-closed curtain. These sensory cues—so often overlooked—lay the foundation for how we feel, how we connect, and how we come alive.

When we talk about healing, intimacy, or even sex, we often start with the mind. What do you think? What do you want? But the truth is, the body often knows first. The senses are the messengers. They deliver the opening lines of an experience long before we consciously recognize what's unfolding.

That flutter in your chest when someone looks at you just so. The feeling of grounding that comes when bare feet meet cool earth. The way a particular song seems to unlock something in you—something you didn't even realize you were holding. These are not just moments. These are sense-memories, mapping a story on your nervous system that becomes the backdrop to everything else.

So, what happens when we tune in on purpose?

When we start to pay attention to the way our body responds to scent, sound, taste, texture, and light, we begin to write new scenes. We edit old ones. We start to notice how cinnamon makes us feel safe, or how soft lighting eases the tension in our shoulders. We realize that the smell of a certain cologne isn't just a smell—it's a tether to desire. That the warmth of a bath isn't just comfort—it's a cue that our body is safe enough to soften.

Sensory awareness is not frivolous. It is foundational. For those healing from trauma or looking to reclaim a sense of agency in their own bodies, the senses can become a portal— not just to pleasure, but to presence. To resilience. To play. To choice.

Because, yes, the body keeps the score. It remembers what was too much, too fast, or not enough. It carries the echoes of every slammed door, every unmet need, every time you overrode your own instincts. But it also holds the potential to feel safe again. To experience joy, arousal, delight—not in some far-off perfect future, but here, in the small details of now.

And that begins with a single sensory cue.

Maybe it's the feel of linen sheets. Or the sound of rain on a window. Maybe it's a bite of dark chocolate or the scent of lavender on your pillow. Whatever it is, it matters. Because every time you notice it, every time you allow your senses to anchor you to something good, you rewrite the story your body tells.

And just like that, the opening scene begins again.

This time, with intention. This time, on your terms.

Scent: The Invisible Trigger

Scent is often called the most *primal* of our senses, and for good reason—it bypasses logic and goes straight to emotion. When you inhale a fragrance, molecules travel through the olfactory system to the limbic brain, which is the center for memory, emotion, and arousal. This is why the smell of a particular cologne, body lotion, or even fresh laundry can evoke powerful feelings or bring you right back to a specific moment (or person) in time.

This link between scent and memory was first recognized in modern psychology by Marcel Proust, whose famous description of a madeleine cake dipped in tea sparked a cascade of memories—a phenomenon now called the *Proustian memory effect*. However, long before that, ancient cultures understood the influence of scent. Egyptians used essential oils in sacred rituals. The Greeks and Romans infused their baths with herbs to relax and arouse. In Ayurveda and Traditional Chinese Medicine, scent has long been used to balance energy and stimulate well-being.

Modern neuroscience confirms what these cultures knew instinctively: Olfaction (the sense of smell) has a direct pathway to the amygdala and hippocampus—areas responsible for emotional memory and survival instincts. In short, what you smell can influence how safe, attractive, or connected you feel in a matter of seconds.

So, whether it's the comforting smell of your partner's T-shirt, a spritz of your favorite perfume, or the rich, earthy scent of sandalwood that grounds you, your nose might just be your most underrated tool for pleasure. You can use scent deliberately: Apply a lotion that reminds you of a good memory, light a candle that evokes calm, or experiment with pheromone-enhanced oils. Although the jury is still out, scientifically speaking, as to whether or not pheromone oils may have an effect on mood or sexual response, using scent can become part of a meaningful ritual or shift in mindset, acting as a "cue" or ritual for intimacy. What matters is the personal association—what wakes up *your* nervous system in the best possible way.

Color: The Quiet Mood Setter

While scent hits like a burst of emotion, color functions more like background music—it sets the tone, often without us noticing. The study of how color influences human perception and behavior is called chromatics, and it's been examined in everything from interior design and advertising to art therapy and neuroscience.

Different colors activate different psychological responses. Warm colors like red, orange, and deep gold are linked to passion, energy, and intimacy. Think candlelight, sun-drenched sheets, or a rosy glow in someone's cheeks after a good kiss. In contrast, cool tones like blue, lavender, and pale green tend to soothe the nervous system, evoking a sense of safety, rest, and introspection. A spa painted in icy gray-blue isn't a random choice—it's a psychological cue for you to exhale.

The origins of color theory can be traced to Johann Wolfgang von Goethe, who in 1810 wrote a treatise on how colors affect human mood and behavior—an idea that would later impact both artists and psychologists. In contemporary research, studies have demonstrated that color can affect everything from heart rate to sexual attraction. Red, in particular, has been shown to boost perceived attractiveness and sexual interest, probably due to its evolutionary links to fertility and vitality.

This means that the environment you create—the sheets you select, the colors on your walls, even the clothes you wear—can all become part of your sensual story. You don't need to redecorate your bedroom to feel a shift. A silky red robe. A pale pink light bulb. A forest green candle flickering in the corner. These are sensory cues, yes, but also invitations.

Color Me Curious: Choosing Colors That Stir the Senses

When it comes to setting the mood, we often think about music, lighting, or scent—but color is one of the most underrated sensual tools we have. Chromatics explores how certain hues can influence our mood, behavior, and even our arousal levels. Think of it as a visual whisper to the nervous system.

Choosing colors intentionally—whether for your bedroom, your lingerie, or even the lighting on a quiet night in—can enhance your connection to sensuality, pleasure, and presence. Some colors activate and awaken. Others soften and soothe. And some seem to do both, depending on how you use them.

Here are a few shades to play with . . .

Red

The classic. Red stimulates excitement, passion, and desire. It increases heart rate and draws attention, making it perfect for moments of bold expression or fiery energy. Want to feel more daring or confident? Add a splash of red—lipstick, lingerie, or even a throw pillow.

Pink

Soft pinks evoke tenderness and affection. It speaks the language of romance, nurturing, and flirtation. Dusty rose, blush, or warm pink shades can make a space feel welcoming, intimate, and emotionally safe.

Coral or Orange

Energetic and creative, orange is a warm, playful color that sparks vitality and engagement. It's a great pick for moments when you want to feel both sexy and alive—think sensual exploration with a lighthearted twist.

Deep Purple or Plum

Purple has long been linked with luxury, mystery, and the erotic imagination. Darker shades suggest depth, fantasy, and the sacred. Ideal for setting a mood that's both grounded and otherworldly.

Teal or Midnight Blue

Cool tones like teal or deep blue calm the nervous system and support emotional openness. They're ideal for when you want to slow down, feel secure, and reconnect with your body or your partner.

Color choices reflect how you want to feel—so be open to experimenting. A silk scarf, a candle, a "feature" painted wall . . . sometimes the smallest splash of color can shift your mood, and your desire.

· · · ·

The Scent of Yes: Aromas That Awaken Arousal

Just as color speaks to the eyes, scent whispers directly to the brain. Scent bypasses logic and travels straight to the limbic system—the part of the brain that governs emotion, memory, and arousal. That's why a familiar perfume can make your heart race or why the warm smell of your partner's skin can feel like home.

Tuning into scent isn't just about fragrance; it's about using olfaction as a gateway to awareness, connection, and turn-on. Here are some scent notes to explore. While not necessarily scientifically proven, many people swear by their ability to awaken the senses in the most pleasurable ways.

Rose, Jasmine, and Ylang Ylang

These floral notes are regarded as natural aphrodisiacs. They foster feelings of romance, sensuality, and emotional openness. Perfect for slow, intentional evenings.

Vanilla and Cocoa

Warm, inviting, and slightly indulgent. These scents evoke trust and pleasure, and studies have shown they can increase sexual arousal—particularly in women.

Sandalwood and Patchouli

Earthy and grounding, these deep notes can evoke intimacy, safety, and depth. Ideal for connecting with your body and calming performance anxiety.

Citrus (Orange, Bergamot, Grapefruit)

Bright and invigorating, citrus scents lift the mood and boost alertness. Think playful, flirty energy. A great choice for mornings—or anytime you need a gentle reset.

Your Partner's Natural Scent

As mentioned above, your partner's natural body scent, especially when you feel emotionally safe with them, can be a powerful, primal turn-on. There's science to back this up: Scent also plays a role in compatibility and sexual chemistry.

Aromas can anchor memories, soothe nerves, or spark new excitement. A spritz of something cherished. A massage oil reserved just for each other. The way the sheets smell after a warm bath. These small choices shape how the body *remembers* pleasure. So the next time you're "not in the mood," try leading with your nose.

Your body just might follow.

Learning to Lead with the Mind

My client Sarah had been experiencing a disconnection from her desires and intimacy with her partner. She came to me feeling stuck in repetitive patterns in her intimate life. She described herself as a passive participant in her own sensual experiences. She shared that she often felt too tired or too bored with her sex life to feel motivated to participate. She said that she felt "boxed in" in her sex life. "It's just uneventful—like it's on repeat."

During our sessions, I introduced Sarah to the concept of mental foreplay. I explained that before our bodies can truly engage, our minds need to lead the way. It's about cultivating an inner landscape where anticipation could flourish and imagination could reignite her desires. Mental foreplay isn't about changing who you are; it's about giving yourself permission to explore new possibilities within.

With my help, Sarah began to envision herself as someone confident, adventurous, and playful—qualities she longed to express but felt had been buried beneath layers of self-doubt and cultural expectations. We also incorporated EMDR (Eye Movement Desensitization and Reprocessing) into our sessions.

EMDR proved invaluable in helping Sarah reprocess past experiences that had shaped her perceptions of intimacy and desire. We also worked on a Future Template exercise, where she imagined positive sexual scenarios filled with confidence and joy, anchoring those feelings with the use of EMDR, so the feelings could become part of her present reality.

As part of this mental rehearsal, Sarah incorporated sensory cues that resonated with her new narrative. She began experimenting with colors in her bedroom—adding soft pinks and warm hues to create an inviting, intimate space. She rediscovered the power of scent with perfumes and oils that made her feel sensual and alive. These small, intentional changes gradually shifted her internal landscape, creating an environment where her desire could unfold more naturally.

Over time, Sarah noticed significant changes in her relationship with her partner and herself. Her imagination had opened doors to an expansive inner world where pleasure wasn't just anticipated—it was crafted, nurtured, and celebrated. She described feeling more present in her body, more connected to her partner, and more liberated to explore the depths of her sexuality.

Through mental foreplay, Sarah didn't just rediscover her sexuality; she reclaimed her right to feel joy in every touch, whisper, and shared gaze.

Chapter 8

It's an Inside Job: Pleasure Starts Within

We often talk about chemistry, connection, and finding the right person, the right spark, the right moment. But when it comes to genuine—and expansive—sexual pleasure, the reality is that it's an inside job.

That doesn't mean it's a solo act (though solo pleasure definitely counts). It means that the foundation of sexual well-being is built within us: in our beliefs, histories, nervous systems, and our ability to feel safe enough to receive. Our past influences our present, whether we notice it or not. Sometimes what we carry isn't even ours to begin with.

Many of us inherited stories about sex and desire that were never truly ours. Maybe your family avoided the topic—and the media provided you with scripts full of performance ideas—but the stories lacked connection to your own life. Generational trauma, religious shame, recurring themes of unworthiness or silence—they don't just disappear; they tend to settle in and become a constant hum of "not enough," "too much," or "don't ask."

That's why this work begins within. Not by doing more, but by gently uncovering. What beliefs have you absorbed? What fears have you inherited? What stories are still playing in your mind about what you deserve, what your partner thinks of you, or what your pleasure *should* look like? And then—what sustains you? What thoughts inspire you? What conditions make you feel safe, seen, and wanted? What helps you move from disconnection to curiosity?

Context is important. So is emotional safety—and feeling like you're not being judged, whether it's about your body, your preferences, or the pace at which you're moving. So yes, it's an internal process, but that doesn't mean you're alone in it. It means you have the power to start from within—to rewrite your stories, challenge shame, and explore the parts of you that long to be seen and loved, including the parts that feel pleasure. Especially those.

Identifying the Things That Get in the Way

Pleasure doesn't appear instantly like a well-trained dog the moment you light a candle or slip into bed—it happens within a framework. For many of us, that includes years—sometimes decades—of emotional clutter, internalized stories, and patterns that are sneakier than a raccoon in your pantry.

Before we can fully embrace pleasure, we need to acknowledge what might be quietly (or loudly) standing in its way. Sometimes it's physical—there are numerous reasons why we put our pleasure aside. But often, the main obstacles aren't in our bodies; they're in our minds.

The first step is to identify these blocks for what they are: stories, habits, and patterns that may have once helped you navigate difficult times—but no longer serve you. Recognizing them doesn't mean beating yourself up. This isn't about blame. You're not a bad partner or a broken person because things feel complicated. You're just human, carrying a lot of history into a very tender part of your life. You might find yourself pulling away just as something starts to feel good. You might freeze instead of speaking up. You might judge your desire before it even has a chance to arrive. These are protective responses—not signs that something's wrong with you, but clues that something inside needs attention.

When you discover what's blocking you, you choose—consciously and lovingly—what to carry forward and what to set down. Pleasure doesn't flourish under pressure; it develops in safety, curiosity, and breathing space.

Fear Masquerading as Logic

We often tell ourselves plausible-sounding stories that conceal emotional fear. "I'm just too tired." "It's not that important to me." "My partner should just know." While all of these might be valid at times, when they become chronic, it's worth pausing to ask: Is this avoidance arising from fatigue—or from fear of vulnerability? Is it truly a lack of interest—or a fear of being seen?

Fear of rejection or not being enough—or of being too much. These are deeply human anxieties, and they're wired into our survival systems. But they can also hinder pleasure, connection, and the willingness to engage in erotic exploration.

Internalized Performance Pressure

For many people—especially women and gender-diverse individuals—there's a strong undercurrent of performative pressure around sex. We internalize societal expectations about what we "should" want, how our bodies should appear, and what sex is "supposed" to be. This pressure can overpower genuine desire. Instead of tuning in, we tune out.

Even positive-sounding ideas like "being a good lover" or "keeping the spark alive" can feel burdensome if they're motivated by obligation instead of mutual enjoyment. Pleasure flourishes through authenticity, not performance.

Past Hurt and Unprocessed Experiences

Whether it's a specific trauma, a series of painful rejections, or subtle moments of not being heard or respected, unresolved experiences reside in the body. They can diminish arousal, tighten the muscles, and make some forms of touch feel unsafe—even if they seem "gentle" or "loving" on the surface. Sometimes, our body says no before our mind even catches up. Pleasure can only flourish when the nervous system feels safe. That safety starts with recognizing what hasn't been released or healed.

Disconnection from Our Own Needs

One of the most common obstacles is our disconnection from ourselves. Many of us spend years (or decades) focusing on what others need from us. We shape-shift, accommodate, and please. Over time, we forget what we want. We forget what pleasure even feels like in our own bodies. We don't know how to ask for it—let alone receive it—because we haven't been taught to tune into our own internal compass.

But awareness changes everything. Once we begin to identify the stories, fears, and patterns that stand in the way, we can begin to unravel them. We can make room for new scripts and start practicing pleasure—not as a performance or duty, but something that belongs to us.

The Echo Chamber: Generational Trauma and Sexual Pleasure

We like to think of ourselves as free agents—deciding what we want, what we don't, and how we'll love or be loved. But here's the catch: We rarely step into relationships or sexual experiences as blank slates. Most of us carry a suitcase or two. Some are vintage hand-me-downs, full of beliefs passed down through generations. Others are more recent—overnight bags packed in a panic, stuffed with past experiences we haven't had time to sort through. And the baggage is not just metaphorical. These inherited beliefs and unexamined fears often infiltrate the bedroom.

Repeated emotional themes can act like invisible scripts. Maybe your mother's silence about pleasure became your own. Or a generational message like "good girls don't" got rewritten into "I'm not supposed to want this," even if the "this" is gentle, loving, consensual, and joyful. These beliefs aren't your fault— but they might still be shaping your sex life in ways you haven't fully noticed.

Fear—particularly the kind rooted in long-standing stories—has a sneaky way of shaping what we expect. If you believe, deep down, that asking for what you want will result in rejection or judgment, you may instinctively shut down the desire altogether. It's a protective response, but it also keeps pleasure at arm's length. Sometimes we lower our expectations, not because our interest has faded, but because we're afraid of disappointment. And once fear sets the scene, we often don't realize we're still acting out the same scene . . . again and again.

But identifying these patterns doesn't require a PhD in family history—or a family confrontation. It begins with curiosity. What beliefs about sexuality were you shown? What words did you hear—or not hear—about pleasure, desire, or boundaries? Whose voices still resonate in your mind when you make choices about sex?

When it comes to identifying patterns, awareness is the secret sauce. Once you identify a pattern, you can question it. *Do I still believe this? Did I ever? Does it serve me? If not, what might I prefer to believe instead?*

Another way to loosen the grip of these old stories is to write new ones—sometimes literally. You can journal, or better yet, write a "future sexual me" story or a sexual recipe (pages 146–148). Visualize a version of yourself unbound by those beliefs and imagine how you would show up in sex and relationships if you truly felt safe, deserving, and seen in the light you desire. That future self might not have all the answers, but she's ready to explore a different ending.

And if the old stories still pipe up from time to time—because they likely will—just know this: Rewriting takes time.

But every time you say yes to pleasure, curiosity, or even rest, you're revising the narrative. You're the author now.

Thoughts, Feelings, and the Spin Cycle of the Mind

Our thoughts are tiny but powerful things. They covertly hiss declarations and suggestions, shaping entire emotional landscapes without our consent. They even lead us into imaginary arguments or situations we haven't experienced yet (and may never). If you've ever lain in bed running through an entire soap opera in your mind—complete with plot twists and dramatic exits—you know exactly what I mean.

When it comes to sex and pleasure, our thoughts play an outsized role. They don't just commentate on what's happening—they often *create* the entire experience. This isn't just poetic; it's neurological. Thoughts trigger emotional responses, and those emotions then feed back into our thoughts. It's a loop, a feedback system, a full-on spin cycle. Depending on what we toss in there, it can feel like a fabulous recipe . . . or a tangled mess of wasted ingredients.

Take this example: You're getting ready to be intimate with your partner. A neutral thought appears—*I feel a little off today.* But then it escalates—*Why do I always feel off? Am I broken? What if they notice I'm not into it? What if they think I don't desire them?* Suddenly, you're not in your body at all. You're in your head, being cornered by inner critics who all sound suspiciously like that one ex who never really understood you.

On the flip side, imagine catching that initial thought and approaching it with curiosity instead of panic. *Hmm. I'm not quite there yet. What might help me shift gears?* That small pivot—a different thought—can invite a completely different emotion—like gentleness and acceptance.

This is where emotional intelligence and sexual well-being intersect. When we become aware of our inner dialogue, we notice which thoughts bring us closer to pleasure—and which ones shut the door. It's not about forcing toxic positivity or pretending everything is perfect all the time; it's about recognizing the stories we tell ourselves—and gently, purposefully, choosing different ones when they no longer serve us.

Sometimes that involves interrupting the narrative mid-sentence. Other times, it's about intentionally creating new, deliberate thoughts. Like setting a mental table for pleasure: *I don't have to be turned on yet. I'm allowed to warm up. This is my body, and I get to go at my own pace.*

Our thoughts can be either the permission slip or the obstacle course. The good news is: With practice, you can train your brain to be a better ally. Because pleasure doesn't start in the genitals—it begins in the space between your ears.

The Desire Spectrum: It's Not a Light Switch; It's a Dimmer (with a Mood Ring)

If only desire were like a light switch—on or off, clear and predictable. But more often, it's like a dimmer—connected to a mood ring . . . changing colors depending on the weather, your stress levels, whether you've eaten, if your inbox is manageable, and if your partner remembered to take the recycling out. In other words, it's complicated.

The truth is, sexual interest and arousal don't operate on a fixed schedule. They exist on a continuum—and that continuum can change daily, hourly, even moment to moment. What feels thrilling one day might feel neutral the next. What you brushed off last month might suddenly seem like an exciting new adventure.

This is where we get tripped up: the assumption that desire should arrive fully formed, like a perfectly ripe mango. But in reality, desire frequently ripens in real time—when we're attuned to context, connection, and emotional safety.

Context is everything. Are you tired? Holding in a passive-aggressive sigh about how your partner loaded the dishwasher like it's a game of Jenga? That context matters. Your brain is the biggest sexual organ you have, and it does a lightning-fast scan of your environment, assessing if the emotional temperature is off. If it is, your libido probably hits the snooze button.

Now include emotional well-being. If your nervous system is flooded—by stress, overwhelm, anxiety—then arousal doesn't get the green light. It's not a malfunction; your body is trying to protect you. Your system is prioritizing survival, not seduction. Desire can't bloom when your brain thinks you're fleeing from a metaphorical bear (even if the "bear" is just a full to-do list and a looming deadline).

This is why it's essential to understand the difference between *spontaneous desire and responsive desire.* Spontaneous desire is that lightning bolt of want that seems to strike unprompted but is more likely triggered by a simple connection—a thought, a touch, or a flirt earlier in the day—that stirs a response. And then there is responsive desire, which is that slow burn that develops once you've started the process of sexual connection. Many women—and people in long-term relationships—experience the latter more often. There's absolutely nothing wrong with needing a little warm-up. That's not low libido; it's part of life. It's not a *no* to sex, but a *maybe* and a need for time to shift or transition, allowing your desire to emerge.

When you realize that pleasure exists on a spectrum—and that it's deeply influenced by emotional context, timing, and relationship dynamics—you can stop blaming yourself for not being "in the mood." Instead, start creating the conditions that allow your desire to emerge.

Maybe that looks like:

> **Revisiting what excites you *now*,** not what did five years ago.
> **Creating micro-moments of connection throughout the day**—a flirty text, a long hug, a shared joke.
> **Tuning into your arousal cues without judgment.** (Dry spells don't necessarily mean something is wrong; they might indicate you're burned out.)

There are countless variables—internal and external—that influence your sexual experience: hormones, medications, relationship satisfaction, how you feel about your body, whether you've had enough sleep or water. It's all interconnected. And no single variable determines your sexuality. Pleasure is dynamic. It changes, expands, and contracts. Some days it's playful, some days shy, and sometimes it's just . . . not present. And that's completely fine.

Don't aim for a fixed state of desire; instead, promise yourself to stay curious. Pay attention and let your arousal be something you discover, not something you force. Your sexual pleasure is not a test to pass—it's a relationship to nurture.

Emotional Safety: The Real Aphrodisiac

If sex were only about anatomy, a diagram would suffice—but it's not. Because the body can't truly relax into pleasure if the heart is bracing for rejection.

Emotional safety is one of the most underrated—and essential—elements in a satisfying sexual life. It's the invisible force field that allows us to soften, to be vulnerable, to try new things without fear of ridicule.

Emotional safety means feeling secure enough to share a need, admit you're uncertain, or laugh while trying something new without fear of criticism or distance. But here's the twist: Emotional safety isn't only about your partner—it's also about you.

Enter: self-judgment.

We often talk about being judged *by* our partner. However, the inner dialogue—what you believe they think about you—can be just as impactful, and sometimes more punishing. *Do they think I'm taking too long? Do I look weird in this position? Am I boring?*

If we pause and reflect, these are the thoughts circulating *in your mind*; it's not your libido that needs attention, but your inner dialogue that requires gentle attunement. Your partner might not be judging you at all. However, if you're already judging yourself, you're filtering every experience through the lens of self-doubt. That filter can completely diminish your capacity for arousal and connection.

Self-judgment can be devious. Sometimes we *pre-reject* ourselves before our partner even has a chance to respond. We expect their disinterest, disappointment, or critical eye—because that's what we've been told, based on old stories and wounds. Maybe someone in the past criticized you. Or you've internalized cultural messages about how you "should" look, act, or feel. Is it possible that you've never been told you're allowed to want more? Cultivating emotional safety starts with listening to your own inner voice.

Ask yourself:

- Do I feel safe in my body at this moment?
- Do I believe I am worthy of pleasure, even if it takes time?
- Can I honestly share with my partner what I want or what I'm uncertain about?

And if you're in a partnership:

- Can you discuss what makes each of you feel safe?
- Are there unspoken assumptions that should be discussed with gentleness and mutual respect?
- Can you foster a shared understanding that sex isn't a performance, but a conversation—with pauses, edits, and (yes) joy?

When we feel emotionally safe, we don't need to perform. We don't have to brace ourselves. We can experiment, change gears, or say, "Actually . . . not tonight," without guilt or fear, and trust that we'll still be loved.

That's when the true magic of sexual connection begins—not just when bodies meet, but when the fear of being "too much" or "not enough" starts to fade. When we stop trying to be perfect and start allowing ourselves to be present.

Chapter 9

Desire Is a Moving Target

If there's one thing certain about human beings, it's this: We are always evolving. Moment to moment, season to season, year to year—nothing about us remains static. Our thoughts shift, our bodies change, and our desires meander. Preferences expand, contract, or do a bit of a sideways shuffle. And yet, despite all this constant change, we're often told that in relationships—especially long-term ones—we should find a comfortable rhythm and stick with it.

There's something seductive about this idea. That once we "know" our partner, we've arrived. That we've done the work. We can set the emotional cruise control and expect things to stay the same. But that's not how people operate, and certainly not how pleasure functions.

The truth is, assuming we know everything about ourselves—or about someone else—isn't just wishful thinking. It's a recipe for disappointment. Desire doesn't fit into a tidy little box, nor do we. The idea that you can fully "figure out" yourself or your partner is a charming myth—but a myth nonetheless.

Assumptions can become traps. When we presume we already know what excites our partner, we stop asking. When we assume we'll always enjoy what we used to like, we stop exploring. When we assume we'll never change, we miss the opportunity to discover something new. Assumptions keep us tethered to the past. Curiosity draws us into the present.

Most of us learn early in life that changing our minds—or our desires—is somehow seen as inconsistent. We believe that once we declare our preferences, we are expected to stick to them. As if growth or change implies unreliability. However, change is not a failure of character; it is *evidence of life*. In fact, remaining the same often indicates that we are avoiding growth, not embracing it.

In the realm of sexuality, these assumptions manifest in many subtle ways. You might think, *I've never liked that*, without realizing that a different context or mood could make it feel completely different. Or maybe you've always started sex in a certain way, and your partner's used to it—but they're craving something else and don't know how to say it. Perhaps you presume your partner isn't into something just because they haven't mentioned it.

But if we're constantly changing, our sexual preferences will evolve as well. The only way to keep pace is to stay open-minded. Ask questions, revisit old favorites, explore new options. And accept that sometimes something that didn't work before might just hit differently now. Or the opposite—something that always worked may no longer inspire anything at all.

Always Becoming: Embracing Change in Ourselves and Each Other

It's worth noting, too, that we're not only evolving sexually, but also emotionally, spiritually, and neurochemically. The cocktail of hormones, memories, and moods that defines us today isn't the same recipe as yesterday's. What fascinated us last summer might not have the same effect this winter—and that's part of human nature.

In long-term relationships, this can be challenging. When two people are both evolving (and perhaps in different ways or at different rates), it can cause friction. But that friction might simply mean it's time for an update. A version 2.0—or 7.3—of who you both are and how you love each other.

This is where the idea of being "a work in progress" becomes so meaningful. Not just as a cliché, but as a guiding principle. It allows us to accept where we are now without needing to justify it by who we were then. It grants us the freedom to try, and to try again. It permits us to say, "This isn't working for me anymore" without needing to explain why. And it offers our partners the opportunity to do the same.

Rather than feeling discouraged by the fact that we are all (constantly) under construction, we can find inspiration in it. It means there's always something new to learn and that your sex life isn't "done." Your capacity for pleasure isn't exhausted, and your relationship hasn't reached its final form. There are still new experiences, new expressions, and new layers waiting to be discovered.

So, what does that look like in practice? It might involve making space for check-ins with yourself and your partner— not just about logistics or plans, but about pleasure. It might mean not assuming that you know what they want tonight just because you knew what they wanted last week. Try noticing your own shifts in desire without judgment or panic. It might mean saying: *"I'm not sure what I want today, but I'm open to discovering it."*

Ultimately, that's what keeps sex—and intimacy—alive: the willingness to show up with curiosity and compassion for who we're becoming, not a fixed routine or a perfect playbook.

Yes, we are all, without exception, works in progress. And that's a beautiful invitation to get curious about what exhilarating discoveries could be around the next corner.

When Desire Changed Its Address

When Lauren turned fifty, she noticed something unsettling: Her body no longer responded the way it used to. Sex had always been a dependable part of her relationship—not always fireworks, but there was rhythm and familiarity. Lately, however, she felt numb. Not emotionally—just . . . physically. As if someone had turned down the volume on her sensations.

At first, she attributed it to age. *This is just what happens,* she told herself. But the thought didn't sit well. Lauren wasn't ready to fade into the background of her own pleasure. She wanted to feel *alive*, not just functional.

Therapy helped her uncover just how long she'd been merely "getting through it." Somewhere along the way—between raising kids, losing a parent, and never truly loving her body—she had become disconnected from herself. Sex had become something she did *with* her partner, not something she experienced *for* herself. So, she decided to start fresh.

Lauren bought a mirror. Not the foggy one in her bathroom, but a full-length mirror she placed in a private space where she could be alone. She started exploring her body with curiosity, not criticism. She noticed how her skin responded to different fabrics, how some parts of her body felt more awake in the morning than at night, and how certain touches took her breath away. She wasn't chasing orgasm. She was seeking *connection*—to herself.

Eventually, she invited her partner into this new process. They slowed down—and changed the script. She guided his hands instead of waiting for him to guess. For the first time, she wasn't just participating in pleasure—she was co-creating it. Lauren hadn't lost her desire. It just moved locations. And now, she finally knew how to find it.

Desire Doesn't Owe You an Explanation

Desire isn't something we conquer or finally get a handle on. It isn't a fixed destination we reach by ticking boxes or following the "rules." It's more like a shifting landscape—a terrain that shifts in response to our bodies, what's happening in our individual lives, and, most definitely, what's in our imagination. Sometimes it announces itself, and sometimes it's just quiet— not gone completely—just quiet.

There's no universal formula, no perfect road map, no one-size-fits-all "fix" for how we feel or why we feel that way. What lights you up today might seem irrelevant tomorrow. What once felt dull may suddenly feel electrifying.

But sometimes, amid school drop-offs, work deadlines, and the comforting blur of a long-term partnership, your sex life can become . . . quiet—like a once-loved song turned down so low you can barely hear it anymore.

The key is not to panic. There may be a straightforward, useful tool to help, and breathwork is one of those options.

Breath as Foreplay

Let's take a moment to demystify what foreplay has been marketed to us as. It's not simply a checklist of kisses, caresses, and timed escalations toward The Main Event. Sometimes, the most powerful form of foreplay doesn't even involve touch at all.

Breath is one of the fastest ways to bring your body—and your mind—into the moment. In a culture of constant movement and multitasking, the simple act of breathing *with* someone can feel surprisingly intimate.

When we breathe slowly and intentionally, we cue our nervous system that we feel safe. Safety is the bedrock of arousal. It's what allows the rest of the system (yes, including your genitals) to even begin to consider pleasure.

Intentional breathing lowers your heart rate, grounds you in your body, and helps clear the mental static that blocks desire. When you sync your breath with someone else's, it deepens your connection to a whole new level. It might feel awkward or silly at first, but once you try it, it cultivates an amplified level of intimacy.

Try This:
Step 1: Get comfortable. Sit facing your partner or lie side by side. No phones or distractions, just presence. You don't have to make eye contact unless you want to.

Step 2: Start to match your breath. Begin breathing slowly in and out—about four counts in, four counts out. Don't worry about perfection. Let it be gentle.

Step 3: Tune in. Notice how your body responds. Maybe your shoulders drop. Maybe your thoughts soften—or you start to feel warmth, or a spark of something else.

Step 4: Stay there. Try for five minutes at first and work up from there.

This is not about turning you into a tantric guru overnight. It's about reminding your body—and your partner's—that pleasure can start in this quiet experience. Readiness is something you can *cultivate*, not something you have to force.

• • • •

Passion isn't something you can pin down or study under glass. It responds to your life, body, stress levels, history, and healing process. Some days it's fireworks, and other days it leaves a sticky note on the door saying, "Not today." It's alive—dependent on context, connection, and change. Instead of thinking it's "lost" or judging it, try following it, deftly, unobtrusively, as if it's something untamed. Sometimes it can be elusive—but it's truly breathtaking when you meet it face-to-face.

Off Script

Caleb, thirty-four, had always been "the agreeable one." He was attentive, kind, and never wanted to rock the boat—especially in bed. His partner, Jade, was more vocal about what they wanted. Caleb, on the other hand, had spent most of his life focused on making *someone else* feel good, unsure of what turned him on.

During therapy, Caleb admitted that he often felt discon-nected during sex, as if he was just playing a role. He hadn't truly explored fantasies or preferences—partly because he feared judgment, but mainly because no one had ever asked.

With time and support, Caleb started exploring what *he* enjoyed. He journaled his fantasies, read erotic stories, and even used guided imagery exercises to connect with bodily signals. What surprised him most was discovering that he enjoyed being in control—something that felt unfamiliar in his daily life. He nervously shared this with Jade, who responded with curiosity rather than rejection.

Caleb and Jade began experimenting with role-play and taking turns planning their sexual encounters. Caleb began to feel present—not because he was doing more, but because he was finally showing up as *himself.*

For the first time in his adult life, sex wasn't just about being good at it. It was about being real.

Exercise: The Flavor of Desire—A Tasting Menu of Your Sexual Evolution

Desire evolves. It simmers, cools, boils over, and sometimes vanishes completely, only to reemerge in unexpected ways—but that doesn't mean it's off the table. This reflection en-courages you to explore the "tasting notes" of your desire over time and observe what ingredients support or inhibit your appetite for connection and pleasure.

Step 1: Sample Past Courses
Think of your sexual journey as a multi-course meal. What were the early flavors? Divide your past into three "courses" or

stages. They don't have to be equal in length—just meaningful to you.

For each course, ask:

What did desire taste like then? (Was it spicy? Barely seasoned? Overcooked by stress?)

____

____

____

What ingredients brought it to life? (Maybe playfulness, confidence, freedom?)

____

____

____

What left a bitter aftertaste or dulled your appetite?

____

____

____

Step 2: Tune In to Today's Palate

What are you hungry for *now*?

____

____

What sensations, experiences, or environments whet your appetite for pleasure?

____

____

____

What blocks it or makes it feel out of reach?

____

____

____

If you had to describe your current relationship with desire as a dish, what would it be?

____

____

____

Step 3: Add Curiosity to the Grocery List

Without pressuring yourself to cook anything right now, create a curiosity list. These are your ingredients to explore. Write down three to five things—sensual, sexual, or emotional—that you're interested in tasting, trying, or feeling. These aren't obligations; they're possibilities. Maybe it's a new kind of touch, a fantasy, a slower pace, or simply more rest.

Optional Garnish

Create a playful "menu" of your turn-ons and turn-offs—things that currently satisfy, things you've outgrown, and things you're open to trying. (And remember, comfort food counts.)

Journal Prompt: What's on the New Menu?

Take a moment to reflect on where you are now in your relationship with pleasure.

What do you crave more of in terms of connection, touch, intimacy, or self-expression?

———————————————

———————————————

———————————————

What feels nourishing right now—and what no longer
suits your tastes?

———————————————

———————————————

———————————————

Are there any new "flavors" you're curious about? Fantasies, dynamics, settings, sensations?

———————————————

———————————————

———————————————

What stories have you told yourself about your
desires—especially the ones that start with "*I shouldn't
. . .*" or "*I'm supposed to . . .*"? Are any of those worth
retiring from your internal cookbook?

———————————————

———————————————

———————————————

And finally, and just as important:

If you were to create a new *recipe for pleasure*—one
that reflects your present moment—what would it
include?

———————————————

———————————————

———————————————

There are no right answers here. Just possibilities, evolving preferences, and a chance to listen to the whispers of your appetite without judgment.

Chapter 10

Zen and the Art of Intimacy: Where Presence, Pleasure, and the Soul Meet

Sometimes we look for answers in the loudest places: the next big breakthrough, the latest self-improvement plan, or the trendy technique that promises to turn your sex life into a three-ring circus. But what if pleasure wasn't all about mastering more techniques—and more about a quiet way of unlearning the pressure to perform and rediscovering the joy of being present?

The spiritual side of sex is not about exotic toys or elaborate rituals. It's about trusting the wisdom of your body, your breath, and your process. True intimacy grows from the kind of spaciousness where you can allow your desire to rise up and meet you.

Simplicity as Sensuality

In Zen teachings, simplicity isn't about removing pleasure—it's about revealing it. It involves clearing away the clutter, noise, and assumptions that intimacy must look a certain way.

When we slow down, something opens. A breath becomes foreplay, or a glance becomes grounding. A single touch, whether deliberate or unrushed, can be an offering. It's quiet—yet fiercely powerful.

It can be . . . spiritual.

You don't need special rituals or rare symbols to connect with a sense of the sacred. I'm not speaking of religion here; I am referring to something that can feel deeply meaningful in a different way. Sometimes, a moment of pleasure can feel luminous—almost reverent—if you become intentional and mindful. You don't need to burn sage or chant mantras—unless those speak to you. What matters more is a stillness and the willingness to stay present with the moment rather than trying to outthink it.

If you've ever been in the middle of a deeply connected, expressive sex experience, you've probably thought: *Whoa . . . this feels bigger than us.* And you'd be right. There *is* something about how bodies can be in sync that creates space for something sacred. Sex, at its most expansive, can feel like a form of communion—not just with your partner, but with something unseen, something timeless. Dare I say, something divine, with each person bringing their own energy into the sacred space.

Taking the route of passionate, no-holds-barred sex can be incredibly satisfying—though fleeting—and it certainly has the potential to lead to orgasm. In fact, those moments can often extend into dozens of seconds of intensity, rather than a blink. But while that fleeting rush has its own beauty, there's another kind of intimacy waiting: a gentle landing between the divine and the deeply human that lives within us.

It turns out, sex isn't just biology. It's not merely mechanics or simply orgasmic pleasure. At its core, sex is a profound human experience—one that can bring us into the present, keep us grounded in our bodies, and lift us to something greater.

We don't often speak of sex as slow and spacious, but it can be just that. The moment of being completely present is a practice of healing, of returning to yourself. It's not something you "study" or try to see if you are "doing it right"—it's about being open and willing to feel. And when you do, something magical can happen. That "magic" lives within breath, closeness, and the significance of those moments when body and spirit touch, and something transformative unfolds.

Yes, sex can be explosive, but it can also be peaceful, expansive, and sacred—you just need to be willing to listen inwardly. To notice the difference between chasing a climax and truly savoring a connection.

Divinity in the Flesh

You arc not just a body navigating the world. You are a living, breathing spark of something much bigger—layered with memory and alive with sensation.

The timeworn saying "we are spiritual beings having a human experience" gets tossed around a lot. But what it really means is that you weren't thrown randomly into this world; you were sculpted by something wise. Call it the universe, God, stardust, source energy—whatever resonates. The truth is, you came here with a blueprint. Not a rigid script, but an enticement to be here, to be real and whole.

And sex is part of that wholeness. Sex is not separate from your spirituality. It doesn't live in a shadowy back room while the rest of your "higher self" meditates. Sex is a sacred ingredient that is at times wild, messy, playful, loud—or serene, peaceful, luxurious, and even transcendent.

When grounded in consent, mutuality, and respect, sex becomes a celebration of life. It's a way of honoring life energy itself—the pulse of creation, the fire in your belly, and the tenderness in your soul.

Intentionality and Sensory Creativity

Think of intentionality as the mise en place of desire. (That's the elegant French phrase for preparing your ingredients before cooking.) It's not about being rigid or overly planned—it's about creating the conditions for pleasure to unfold with ease.

You don't need to choreograph the entire evening. However, incorporating creative sensory play—using soft fabrics, lighting that flatters rather than exposes, music that stirs rather than distracts—can do wonders for the nervous system. You're not seducing someone into a role; you're inviting them to enjoy the moment with you.

Remember, your imagination is a tool. It's not frivolous; it's the foundation of a more fulfilling and sacred connection with your partner. The mind is often where arousal begins. Don't underestimate the power of a mental image, lingering anticipation, or even savoring your own desire before acting on it.

You have the power to decide how to frame this part of your life. You can choose to see your body as sacred and your pleasure as worthy. You can view your partner not as a task to manage or a puzzle to decode—but as someone who also holds the divine within.

That doesn't mean you'll always feel turned on or connected. It simply means that you approach them (and yourself) with reverence.

Try this: Next time you look at your partner—pause. Really pause. Not to fix or change or judge. Just to *see* them. The curve of their back. The way their laugh makes you feel. Take in the warmth of their presence. And then, maybe silently, maybe in your mind, or out loud, say: *I see you. I choose you in this moment.* Because when you shift the frame, everything inside it becomes art.

Sacred Sex

Each person has a private, inner design for what feels good—not only physically but also emotionally, energetically, and spiritually.

You might think you want more "heat," only to find you're actually longing to feel seen. You might seek novelty, only to realize that what you truly need is emotional safety. Or you might understand that you've outgrown the roles and routines that once defined you—and now you're craving something with more heart, and especially more soul.

This is the space where sexuality and spirituality converge—not in a prescriptive or mystical manner, but in a profoundly personal one. It's where your soul gets a seat at the table. And no, this doesn't mean abandoning the fun, the play, or the edge—it simply means giving yourself permission to redefine what excites you.

However, it's not always clear. Sometimes we long for something, only to find ourselves a little disappointed when it doesn't nourish us the way we imagined. This is where self-awareness becomes essential.

Trusting the Energy Within

The truth is, your body already knows a great deal—about what you need, what you're ready for, and what makes you feel safe, open, and powerful.

But sometimes, old beliefs, past experiences, or generational stories hijack those signals, as we've explored in previous chapters. We learn to ignore our "yeses" and silence our "noes," and then we shrink, defer, or disappear—and sometimes, we even forget we're allowed to receive.

Energetic intimacy—the kind that grows through presence and attunement—isn't just spiritual talk. It's a delicate dance between your inner world and outer experience. When you cultivate emotional safety within yourself, it shows in your relationships as well. You stop seeking approval and instead focus on aligning with your true self.

Find a quiet moment. Sit or lie down in a comfortable position and take a moment to slow down.

Listening for Your "Yes" and "No"

1. **Bring something simple to mind.** Imagine holding a warm cup of tea or your favorite food. Notice what your body does. Do your shoulders soften? Does your chest feel open? This is your body's version of a *yes*.

2. **Now, bring to mind something you dislike.** It could be a smell, a taste, or even a task you dread. Notice how your body responds—maybe a tightening in your jaw, a slight pulling back. This is your body's version of a *no*.

3. **Practice with real choices.** As you move through your day, pause with small decisions: Do I want to say yes to this invitation? Does this touch feel welcome? Pay attention to the subtle signals—leaning into something, softening, tightening, or pulling away.

4. **Journal what you notice.** Write down where your yeses and noes show up most clearly. Over time, you'll build trust in your body's cues, even when your mind wants to override them.

Where the Mind Goes, Pleasure Follows

Guided meditations can be powerful tools—not because they give you answers, but because they create space. Space to reconnect with your body. To soften old patterns and breathe into new possibilities.

This next section is a gentle guided meditation—one you can do sitting, lying down, or even during a mindful bath. It's not meant to transport you to some other realm (though that's welcome, too). It's meant to bring you back to yourself. To what's already simmering inside you, the sweetness that comes with stillness and the power of simply being present.

So go ahead—get cozy. Dim the lights if you'd like. Maybe light a candle or grab a soft blanket. Then, when you're ready . . . let your breath lead the way.

Guided Imagery Meditation

Note: The following meditation can be used for relaxation, body awareness, and breathing, mind–body connection, sensation attunement, and releasing held thoughts.

Born from a doctoral research study on women's sexual dissatisfaction and low desire, this guided meditation blends science and mindfulness to awaken what was once dormant.

The results of the study spoke for themselves—renewed desire, greater self-connection, and a more vibrant sense of pleasure. (You may choose to record these words in your own voice or that of a loved one and play it back—or use the link at the beginning of this book to obtain the full meditation recording on my website.)

Begin by sitting in a chair or on your bed, in such a way that you can become totally relaxed and comfortable. Shift your body so you feel fully supported, with your neck, head, and spine aligned.

There is pleasure and comfort in enjoying the feeling of letting go and relaxing. For just a few moments, allow for a free and clear space, a place of stillness just for you. This is a time for you to refresh, to let go.

So now . . .

Allowing yourself to settle into your space, gently close your eyes and just think of yourself becoming more and more relaxed. You may want to place one hand on your heart and one hand on your abdomen, if this is comfortable to you.

Gently concentrate on your breathing, inhaling through your nose and exhaling through your mouth. Breathe deeply down into your body.

So now, breathing in slowly, hold and release very slowly. And again, breathe in slowly, holding and releasing very slowly.

Allow your breathing to return to a natural rhythm and perhaps set your hands in your lap. Notice any sensations in your body and let go of all the tension and stress, blowing out with each breath.

With each beautiful breath, gather up all the unneeded tension and concerns, and breathe it out of your body with each exhale. Just watch and notice your breath with friendly, loving awareness.

If any unwelcome thoughts come into your mind, simply notice the thoughts and send them out, away with the breath. Perhaps place them in a bubble and just allow them to drift away, out of your mind, out of your body, out of your consciousness, floating away with the breeze, into the distance . . . Watch them disappear over the horizon.

Imagining allows for all that you want to feel and be to come to you. What you imagine will eventually become reality . . . for your intuitive mind believes what you imagine; it is malleable and awaits your every word—so just gradually turn your attention inward, toward yourself, and focus on what it is that you want to feel . . . whatever it is that you desire.

Notice what it is that you're physically and emotionally feeling within yourself. As you breathe in, you are replacing any tension and discomfort with clean, fresh air and energy. Naturally and with ease.

There's no need to force it. Just imagine. See your body becoming very calm and at rest, allowing yourself to sink further into the surface that your body rests upon.

Now take a mental exploration through your body so that you can connect to the amazing aesthetics that are all yours. Focus on each part of your body and invite the release and relaxation to come in, in its own way.

Release yourself to the process of letting go and letting your hard-working body rest . . . Give yourself permission to explore . . . Allow your natural interest in yourself to grow. You are safe and this is an experience of comfort. Remember, you are always in control.

Now turn your attention to the subtle sensations of warmth moving all the way through you . . . through every vein, every muscle, cleansing you and giving you life.

Feet

Begin with your feet and think of them getting very heavy. Invite your feet to relax and let go of any tension that they may be holding on to, releasing, allowing your feet to become heavy, sinking down. And then become aware of your toes, each of your lovely toes. Simply imagine all the tension flowing out of your feet and becoming very loose and smooth.

Legs

As you allow the relaxation of your feet and toes to deepen, bring your attention to the muscles of your legs, muscles that do so much work for you every day. Unknot, lengthen, warm, and let the tension leave your legs.

Hips

Now invite your hips to join in. Focus on your hips, letting go of any tension . . . Notice the relaxing sensations, and allow for comfort.

Back

Let's check in with your back muscles and imagine all the muscles relaxing. Imagine each vertebra being warmed and relaxing deeply, lengthening and decompressing any pressure, loosening.

Pelvic Area / Sexual Areas

Notice the tension that you may be holding in your pelvic area and the sexual areas of your lower body . . . allowing that area of your body to release and joyfully just be. Allowing your body to go deeper and becoming more comfortable in the relaxation, this part of your body becoming more relaxed and at ease.

Abdomen

Many of us also hold stress and tightness in our abdomen, often without realizing it. So now is a time to allow that tightness, held within, to dissipate and be free. This is a time for you to be comfortable within your body and within your mind.

Chest and Organs

And then release and relax the muscles of your chest, allowing your heart to expand, to feel nurtured and the organs and tissue within your chest and rib cage to release easily, deeply, comfortably, sinking down a little bit more.

Shoulders

Go to your shoulders, between your shoulder blades and all the way down your arms. Let go and unwind, dropping slightly, letting go of any held worries and the weight of the day. Relax the muscles of your shoulders and arms.

Wrist and Hands/Fingers

Relax your wrists, your hands, your fingers. Is there any tension in these small, delicate muscles? Allow the tension to release.

Neck

Notice any tension that you may be holding in the muscles of your neck, the muscles that hold up your head all day. Mentally trace around your neck, and as you do, imagine the muscles responding to the ease of relaxation and smoothing away all efforts.

Jaw/Head/Scalp/Face

Relax any tension that you may be feeling in your jaw, your face, all the way up to your scalp . . . loosening the muscles, allowing your cheeks and your jaw to relax.

Allow all the muscles around your eyes to let go and imagine a pleasant sense of softening, warming, and a flowing down through your face. Like the gentlest, most loving caress.

Overall Body

Move down your body now, from the top of your head, down your neck, down your shoulders, all the way down your body, appreciating the power and vitality of your beauty . . . grateful for your capacity for healing and renewal—strong and steady and resilient. Identify any remaining traces of tension and let it go; let it flow out.

Allow yourself to have this . . . this comfort and peace. When you feel relaxed, your body begins to heal itself and become energized for the activities you want to pursue. There is a very pleasant and comfortable deep sense of relaxation now.

Your body is kissed by perfection and enjoys being alive, filled with gratitude for just being.

Everything has become quiet and still, and so now take a few moments, just to enjoy the deep, relaxed state of body and mind. Your mind is capable of imagining, creating, and enhancing whatever it desires, whatever it directs attention to and interest to . . . The mind is the most creative, sensual part of each of us, and all of your body responds to what the mind thinks, envisions, and chooses to believe.

Continue to relax in this way for a few more moments, allowing yourself to have this worry-free space, allowing your body to heal and naturally rejuvenate, as it instinctively knows how to do.

Now, imagine a place where you feel safe and at peace, a sanctuary just for you. This can be a place that you have been to before, a place you have always wanted to go, or a created, imagined place. Perhaps a place where you have experienced pleasure and enjoyment. Maybe a secluded spot on an exotic island beach or the mountains. Perhaps floating through the air, light and free. This is a place where you can be free, fully alive, comfortable and healthy. Wherever you want to go that calls to you and provides for a deep sense of peace.

This beautiful, enchanted, serene place is where your mind can be calm, and slow down, where the mind and body can connect. Protected and free from feelings of anxiety, worry, or guilt. Everything is taken care of and the business of the world is shut out for a while. Any anger or resentment is just washed away, cleared away. There is nothing that you must do—just be at peace.

In this place, you are surrounded by an abundance of light, flowing into you and filling you with energy. Enter this place as if walking through a doorway, into your special realm . . . gently closing the door as you enter and leaving the world behind for just a little while.

Release yourself to this moment, to this place. Allow yourself to notice these sensations. This is a place where no shame or hurt exists. Maybe you are holding onto some unwanted thoughts or feelings of guilt or perhaps feelings of unworthiness in receiving love and pleasure. Many people do, but now is a time to let go of those thoughts and feelings . . . to float away—they are not necessary and are only beliefs that you unintentionally picked up along the way, but they do not serve you. So send them away. Release them—it's okay to let them go.

This is a place where you can always come to, a place to reflect, to let yourself use the powers of your imagination, for exploration, for quiet, for healing and learning.

Notice your sensations and notice a pleasant, energizing feeling filling the space around you. These feelings contain excitement and a sense of optimism. A sense that something wonderful is about to happen. It is good and right for you to be here. There is magic in this place—it settles around you . . . Notice the glow in the air.

There is light here that illuminates everything it touches, with exquisite brightness . . . vibrant color . . . all the love and sweetness that has ever been—every good wish is in this place and surrounding you.

Sound/Hear

Listen to the sounds—what do you hear? Are there sounds of water, birds? Is the wind blowing through the trees? Or is there only the sound of stillness? Just enjoy—it's all here for you.

Sight/See

See this place, in your mind's eye . . . look all around. What do you see? Taking it all in as it develops and evolves . . . enjoy the qualities of this space . . . all the details. Look to your right, look to your left, look up to the sky now and toward your feet. Where do your feet rest? Notice yourself as you move through this space. You can feel the air . . . dancing with energy . . . with a sense of gentle wonder.

Look at yourself . . . See how beautiful you are. You are made to be loved, to be sexual and to be appreciated just as you are. Your body is naturally created for loving and pleasure. Your creative mind is overflowing with an abundance of erotic and enjoyable ideas for sexual touch and pleasure. Allow for the space to expand, to make room for your ideas . . .

There is warmth, softness in your heart . . . waves of nurturing, of love . . . soothing away any torn or tender places.

You are magnetic, attractive, and loving. You are a magnificent lover and can be satisfied. Allow for the waves of pleasure to wash over you.

Breathe in fully and deeply, sensing your strength and steadiness, noticing how resilient and relaxed you are.

You are in tune with your body, your vibrant, healthy, and energized body. Send that excellent energy all the way to the base of your spine, then let it travel slowly all the way up your spine to the top of your head, awakening your creative, confident energy. And now, breathing deeply, let it fill your whole body with this generous, healing energy . . . releasing any remaining doubts, insecurities, or fears—melted away, to unveil your erotic, sensual self.

You feel the warmth of this awareness begin to collect and radiate through your entire body, sending compassion and reassurance to every corner of your being . . . As you breathe, breathe into the open spaces of your heart, feeling them expand . . .

Smell/Fragrances

Are there fragrances in the air? Notice them. Notice the caress of the subtle fragrances and aromas. Enjoy the perfect harmony.

Touch/Feel/Textures

Feel the textures of this space . . . What is the temperature of the air? Feel it on your skin . . . Allow your body to move in the ways it wishes to, feeling carefree. Imagine taking the time to gently touch and feel your skin, sliding your hands along your arms, your face, touching and noticing how the caress feels. Perhaps running your fingers through your hair and concentrating on the response of your touch. Allow your body to stretch and expand in this most relaxing way.

Know that you are naturally sensual, sexual, and feminine. Believe in your intentional and thoughtful sexual expression and sexual drive, for your own pleasure and your erotic enrichment. Give yourself permission to explore, imagining your erotic and enjoyable images . . . Receive sensual pleasures— your body was meant to receive and enjoy . . . All of you was made for this—this beauty, these sensations . . . Enjoy how they feel, enjoy envisioning the erotic images . . . to hear, to see, and to feel in this moment.

(Pause for imagination to develop.)

Just enjoy and immerse yourself in the erotic energy flowing through you, through your entire body. Allow all the good feeling sensations of this place to expand within.

Trust in yourself and your true desires and your willingness to receive pleasure and generously love. Give yourself permission to explore . . . Be open to and honor what appeals to you—whatever it is, it is good and right for you.

And now, knowing that you can always come to this place, a place of empowerment, of sensuality, you can always return by simply allowing yourself to recall this place and all the good it provides for you.

When you are ready, you will begin to slowly move toward your awake state. Allow yourself to return by breathing deeply and exhaling deeply . . . and feeling grateful for your ability to relax, to imagine.

Know that you have an increased understanding of yourself in a very tangible way. You have an open heart and mind, feeling love and peace, perhaps forgiveness where needed . . . feeling so good to be you. Feeling surrounded by an abundance of unconditional love and peace.

Take a deep, full, energetic breath . . . You might feel that something powerful has happened . . . a shift has occurred . . . and will continue to occur . . . with or without you consciously working on it. This is a new chapter in your life, of timeless acceptance and a freedom to enjoy. You know with your whole heart . . . with your whole being . . . that all the love that you have ever felt, at any time, is alive and well . . . rich and nourishing and boundless—always available to sustain you. You are connected to your life and your body in a new way now . . . perhaps inspired. Any discomforts have been softened—this has become a part of the depth and richness and texture of your life.

And so, knowing that you can return to this place whenever you wish, and whenever you are ready, very gently and with soft eyes . . . come back into the room. Breathing in and out, slowly open your eyes and return to your awake state. And once more, take a beautiful breath of life.

About the Author

**Certified Expertise in Emotional, Relational,
and Sexual Health**

Dr. Tiffany Stanley is a board-certified psychotherapist, AASECT-Certified Sex Therapist, and Licensed Professional Counselor-Supervisor. She holds a master's in counseling and a Doctorate in Clinical Sexology and has specialized for more than twenty years in sexual health, relationship therapy, and general psychotherapy for adult women, men, and couples. Her private practice is located in Austin, Texas.

Education & Credentials

PhD, Clinical Sexology—American Academy of
Clinical Sexology
Licensed Professional Counselor–Supervisor (LPC-S)
Diplomate—American Board of Sexology
AASECT Certified Sex Therapist
AASECT Board-Certified Clinical Sexologist
Emotionally Focused Therapy (EFT) Trained Therapist
Eye Movement Desensitization and Reprocessing
(EMDR) Trained Therapist

Internal Family Systems (IFS) Trained Therapist
Adult ADHD Trained Therapist

Experience

Dr. Tiffany Stanley is a Texas-board-approved licensed psychotherapist and supervisor and an internationally certified clinician with advanced training across multiple evidence-based therapeutic modalities, including Emotionally Focused Therapy (EFT), Eye Movement Desensitization and Reprocessing (EMDR), and Internal Family Systems (IFS). She is also trained as a Heal Your Life™ Workshop Leader, based on the work of Louise Hay.

For over two decades, she has specialized in supporting adult individuals and couples navigating challenges related to desire and intimacy, female sexual pain conditions such as vaginismus and dyspareunia, orgasmic difficulties, performance anxiety, erection issues, and the emotional and relational impact of infertility. She also provides general psychotherapy for concerns such as anxiety, depression, stress, and self-esteem. Clients describe her approach as warm, knowledgeable, empowering, and deeply supportive.

Beyond her clinical practice, Dr. Stanley is an active researcher, educator, and public speaker. She has been featured on podcasts, panels, and professional events both nationally and internationally, speaking on topics including sexual dysfunction, intimacy after cancer, and her well-regarded sensory-focused guided imagery treatment program for sexual concerns.

In addition to her therapy practice, she develops and leads educational workshops and relationship programs, including the Wise Woman Extreme Self-Care Workshop, The Connected Couple: From Disconnection to Intimacy, and Couples Sex and Intimacy.

Appendix

SCENT/OLFACTION

Scent can act as a trigger for relaxation and arousal. Scent and memory are closely linked through the brain's limbic system, particularly the amygdala and hippocampus, which process emotion and memory. The olfactory bulb has direct connections to these areas, unlike other senses.

COLOR/CHROMATICS

Color psychology explores how different hues influence emotions and behavior. Warm colors such as red and orange are associated with arousal and passion, while cooler colors like blue and green promote relaxation and a sense of calm.

HISTORICAL/CULTURAL REFERENCES

In his 1810 work *Theory of Colours*, Goethe noted the emotional effects of different hues on the soul.

Johann Wolfgang von Goethe believed that colors had intrinsic emotional qualities—yellow evoked warmth and cheerfulness, red passion and energy, while blue expressed calm and longing.

References:

Elliot, A. J., & Maier, M.A. (2014). Color psychology: Effects of perceiving color on psychological functioning in humans. *Annual Review of Psychology*, 65, 95-120. https://www.annual-reviews.org/content/journals/10.1146/annurev-psych-010213-115035

Goethe, J. W. von. (1810). *Theory of Colours*. Translated by Charles Lock Eastlake, 1840. MIT Press edition, 1970.

Herz, R.S. (2004). A naturalistic analysis of autobiographical memories triggered by olfactory, visual, and auditory stimuli. *Chemical Senses*, 29(3), 217-224. https://academic.oup.com/chemse/article-abstract/29/3/217/321318?redirectedFrom=fulltext